The
New Quay
Lifeboats

New Quay: Dylan Thomas's 'cliff-perched town at the far end of Wales'

The New Quay Lifeboats

One hundred and fifty years of service and courage

By Roger Bryan

Published by Llanina Books 2014

ISBN 978-09567199-5-9

Set in Adobe Garamond 11pt on 14pt and Gill Sans Regular

www.rogerbryan.com
www.llaninabooks.com
www.rnli.org

This book can be purchased at the RNLI, Glanmor Terrace, New Quay,
Ceredigion, SA45 9PS, and at www.llaninabooks.com

Cover picture: Morlais Davies
Page ii picture: Roger Bryan
Picture on this page: Unknown holidaymaker

Printed and bound in Wales at
Gomer Press, Llandysul, Ceredigion SA44 4JL

Contents

Foreword by Roger Couch, Lifeboat Operations Manager

THE pleasant recollection of the tranquil, hot summer of 2013, contrasting with the violent storms of January and February 2014, demonstrates very clearly how the power of the weather can affect all our lives. Those of us who live here are very aware of the seasonal onset of high winds and rain but most summer visitors to New Quay, enjoying the sun and the beaches, walking the coast path with its magnificent sea views, do not realise how dangerous these places can be when the weather suddenly changes for the worse.

It was no accident that a lifeboat station was placed here in 1864; New Quay had a thriving fishing industry and was a busy merchant maritime port and shipbuilding centre. Today, 150 years later, the main seagoing activities have changed, concentrated around leisure. The RNLI has been quick to adapt to this change, developing faster, purpose-built lifeboats with all the latest technology to react appropriately to every imaginable weather condition and type of casualty. Lifeguards, sea safety and flood rescue have all extended the lifesaving capabilities of the service.

What the RNLI has not changed is the purpose and values of this charitable organisation – saving lives at sea. The volunteer ethos – selfless, dependable, trustworthy, courageous – the core components for our volunteers, remains steadfast.

The boats might be different, the training and required expertise different, but the people involved with the service today still maintain those same values and beliefs as their predecessors have done since 1864.

To quote from Winston Churchill's speech at the RNLI's Centenary Dinner in 1924, the lifeboat service 'drives on with a courage which is stronger than the storm'. It continues to drive on with its volunteer crews and with its funding still coming from the public.

Since 1864 the lifeboats stationed at New Quay have saved over 344 lives and rendered assistance in many different ways. New Quay provides one of the safest harbours in Cardigan Bay, situated between the lifeboat stations at Aberystwyth and Cardigan, both equipped with Atlantic 85 inshore boats and the flanking ALB stations at Barmouth in the north and Fishguard in the south. New Quay continues to remain an important, strategic location for the RNLI with the Mersey Class all weather lifeboat covering a massive area of Cardigan Bay out into the St. George's Channel, and the inshore lifeboat providing vital cover along the coastline. In celebrating 150 years of our unbroken presence here, we can be proud of the high standard of service that has been established. All credit for this must go to the dedicated lifeboat crews, shore crews and officials, past and present, and the hope that future generations will continue to emulate them.

To conclude, on behalf of all who are connected with the Lifeboats in New Quay, I must thank Roger Bryan for his voluntary time, tenacity, dedication, patience and skill in researching the material for the book and producing such an excellent volume in commemoration of our 150th anniversary. Similarly, sincere thanks to the management and staff at Gomer Press for their help and fine printing skills in bringing it all to fruition.

Acknowledgements

A host of people have helped me with the book, and I thank them all. Everyone in New Quay and at the Lifeboat Station has been extremely helpful, but there are two people I must single out.

Roger Couch, Lifeboat Operations Manager, has been a constant source of help, advice and support, and Station Mechanic Ben Billingham has uncomplainingly assisted me in many ways. Both have been very generous with their time. Thank you.

I owe a great debt to Jeff Morris, author of The Story of the New Quay (Dyfed) Lifeboats. Mr Morris has been Honorary Archivist of the Lifeboat Enthusiasts' Society for more than 30 years, and written and produced 184 books on various aspects of lifeboat history.

A big thank you to former Coxswain Winston Evans, BEM, and present Coxswain Daniel Potter, who between them have 49 years experience as Coxswain and who have been ever willing to share their wealth of knowledge and experience. Researching the book, Winston was described to me as New Quay Royalty; Daniel Potter describes him as a legend.

Former crew member Morlais Davies took the headshots of the 2014 Team, and the wonderful picture for the cover. Thank you.

The management committee was very supportive, especially Alan Tomkins and Glyn Griffiths. Trevor Evans, who has to date completed 47 years of service at the station, was a great help along with crewmen Bernie Davies, Rees-Tom Jones and Jolyon Quayle. Mervyn Thomas's widow Anne was enormously helpful in tracking down photographs. Thank you. The Rev Matthew Baynham, Trevor Davies, Tina Couch and Roger Sims expertly read the proofs, but all mistakes are mine.

At the RNLI Archives in Poole, Barry Cox and Peter Morman were extremely helpful, along with Elise Chainey, Karen Harris, Nathan Williams, Cheryl Frost and Katrina Mallaburn. Nigel Millard and Nicholas Leach were generous with their advice.

Sue Passmore is always the first port of call for anyone researching New Quay. Special thanks to Stuart Evans at Ceredigion Museum, Aberystwyth, for his help and for the lino print of the Nelson; Nia Richards at Ceredigion Library; Helen Palmer and her team at Ceredigion Archives; and staff at both reading rooms at The National Library of Wales, Aberystwyth, and also Mark Davey and his team in the reprographic department. Peter Davis, who has an enormous collection of postcards of Cardiganshire, was as knowledgable as usual.

The local RNLI branches at St Albans, especially Brian Doble, and at Stourbridge, especially Sue Coombes, have assisted me greatly and I thank them both for their original research. Roger Logan at the Foresters archive was also very helpful.

Other people who deserve a mention include Grant McKee, and local photographer Emyr Rhys Williams. Also my daughter Hannah Bryan and her partner Matthew Weeks for their design work on the service records at the back of the book. Gomer Press were even more supportive than normal, especially Gari Lloyd and Pît Dafis.

Every effort has been made to establish copyright on pictures and I apologise for any errors or omissions.

And finally (again) thanks to my wife Bethan for her patience.

Roger Bryan, Plas Llanina, February 2014

Dedicated to those men and women who go out in lifeboats in all weathers ignoring the risks involved; to those who provide the back-up necessary to ensure an efficient service; to the countless thousands who provide the financial support to keep the RNLI afloat; and to those left waiting behind.

AT A MEETING OF THE TRUSTEES OF THE

ROYAL NATIONAL LIFEBOAT INSTITUTION

HELD ON THE 6TH DAY OF NOVEMBER 2013
THE FOLLOWING MINUTE
WAS ORDERED TO BE RECORDED ON THE
BOOKS OF THE INSTITUTION THAT THE
ROYAL NATIONAL LIFEBOAT INSTITUTION
GRATEFULLY RECOGNISES
150 YEARS' SERVICE OF THE

NEW QUAY LIFEBOAT STATION

FROM 1864 TO 2014
IN THE GREAT CAUSE OF
LIFE SAVING FROM DISASTER AT SEA AND DESIRES
TO ACKNOWLEDGE WITH WARM APPRECIATION
THE VOLUNTARY COMMITMENT OF THE LOCAL
LIFEBOAT COMMUNITY AND THE DEDICATION
AND COURAGE OF THE COXSWAINS, HELMS AND
CREWS WHO HAVE NEVER FAILED
TO MAINTAIN THE PROUD TRADITIONS OF
THE LIFEBOAT SERVICE.

CHAIRMAN   PRESIDENT   CHIEF EXECUTIVE

The vellum commemorating 150 years of service at New Quay Lifeboat Station from 1864 to 2014, presented to the Station by the Royal National Lifeboat Institution in 2014.

Forester/Nelson

N THE middle of the 19th century, New Quay was a maritime centre of some importance. Shipbuilding was at its height; around 1860, it was not unusual to see 40 ships in the harbour with as many as ten vessels being built in the shipyards round the bay. The fishing fleet was still active and after the building of the pier in 1835, New Quay had become a busy trading port. Added to this was the number of master mariners that New Quay produced, reputed to be more than any other seaside town in Wales in proportion to its population.

The eminent Welsh maritime historian J Geraint Jenkins could describe New Quay as 'the best example, arguably in the whole of Wales, of a community whose life was completely tied up with the sea.'

The catalyst for the establishment of a lifeboat station at New Quay was the Royal Charter Storm on October 25, 1859. The storm was so-called because the steam clipper Royal Charter, one of the largest ships afloat, on its way from Melbourne, Australia, to Liverpool, was wrecked off the east coast of Anglesey near Moelfre with the loss of more than 450 lives. Many of the passengers were gold prospectors returning home with their treasure – it is estimated that gold bullion and coins worth £80million at today's prices sank beneath the waves, never to be seen again.

The Royal Charter Storm was one of the most severe of the 19th-century, with a death toll of more than 800, and its effect reverberated throughout the British Isles. More than 250 ships were wrecked on the British and Irish coasts during the storm and many others damaged. At New Quay, the Pepper Pot, a much-loved lighthouse at the end of the pier, built in 1839, was completely washed away and many boats in the harbour were damaged.

In 1824, Sir William Hillary had founded the National Institution for the Preservation of Life from Shipwreck and 30 years later, in 1854, this was to become the Royal National Lifeboat Institution. A new design of lifeboat – the self-righter – was being developed and with public appeals making funds available, more lifeboat stations began to be established.

The Inspecting Commander of the Coastguard for the area, Capt JB Ballard RN, petitioned the RNLI on behalf of the residents of New Quay pleading the need for a lifeboat…

'there having been 13 wrecks in the area in the previous seven years with considerable loss of life'. The RNLI's management committee, chaired by Thomas Chapman FRS, agreed to the petition in June, 1864, and tenders were invited for the construction of a boathouse.

The lifeboat station was sited at the top of a steep slope at the end of South John Street, and a powerful winch was needed to haul the lifeboat back uphill to the station. The old boathouse is still in use today and is, among other things, a public shelter.

The first lifeboat allocated to the station was not entirely new – the boat had served at Holyhead for six years and underwent a tortuous journey before arriving at New Quay. She had originally been built by Forrestt, of Limehouse, London, 30ft x 7ft 6in, a ten-oared self-righter costing £161-1s-0d. This was the second of the lifeboats at Holyhead and neither was ever named (a practice not uncommon at the time).

In 1864, she was taken by rail from Holyhead to the boatyard of Woolfe & Son, of Shadwell, London, where she was lengthened by five feet nine inches to 35ft 9in to accommodate 12 oars, effectively making her a new boat.

At the Ancient Order of Foresters Friendly Society's annual national delegates' conference at

The silver plate affixed to the back of the glass cabinet (opposite) is inscribed: 'Model of the Lifeboat NELSON stationed at New Quay Cardiganshire, under the management of the Royal National Life Boat Institution. This model was presented by the Institution to the Donor through Henry Waterfield Esq 1872'. The lifeboat was appropriated to a gift of £680 from an anonymous Lady.

A model of the *Nelson* 1872 held at Ceredigion Museum, Aberystwyth, and on loan to the New Quay Heritage Centre. On the old pulling and sailing lifeboats, the oars on the port side were painted white, and those on the starboard side blue, as can be seen in the model. In confined spaces, before the boat was out in open water where the rudder could be used, if the coxswain wanted to turn to starboard (right) he would call: 'Pull White'. The oarsmen on the port side would start pulling under the instructions of the coxswain and the starboard oarsmen would feather their oars. The boat would steer to the right. And vice-versa if the coxswain wanted to turn to port.

Courtesy of Ceredigion Museum

Shrewsbury in 1862, a proposal was made for a compulsory levy of one penny on all members to support the RNLI 'in aid of their humane and philanthropic institution'.

This was voted down in favour of a voluntary subscription, but the flame had been lit. During 1863, further donations were made to the Voluntary Lifeboat Fund (the first of its kind) and at the 1864 AGM at Halifax, the Executive Council reported that it had been able 'to remit the handsome sum of £255-11s-3d to that noble institution for a Life Boat to be named The Forester. It is our earnest hope that she will never founder for the want of funds to keep her in repair, in guarding the coast of our native shore, and in saving the lives of those who sail on the mighty deep'.

This was the start of the Foresters' long association with the RNLI, who exhibited *Forester* at the AOF's annual fête at Crystal Palace in August, 1864. According to The Foresters' Miscellany of October 1864, 'It was an object of much interest and attraction'.

The journal of the RNLI, The Lifeboat, reported in 1865: 'The National Lifeboat Institution has established a new lifeboat station in the small harbour of New Quay, on the coast of Cardiganshire, in compliance with the wish of the people of the locality to be provided with a lifeboat.

'As the boat would have to be used under sail chiefly, a large 36ft lifeboat has been forwarded to this station. A substantial house has been erected for the boat and a powerful winch to haul the boat up to the house, which is built at the top of a long incline at a considerable height above the water, that being the only practicable spot available.

'The Ancient Order of Foresters have contributed £260 to pay the expense of this life-boat, which is called the *Forester*. The London and North Western and the Cambrian Railway Companies readily took the boat to Aberystwyth, the nearest point of railway to Newquay, and the boat was sailed and rowed from thence to its station'.

In addition to paying for the cost of the lifeboat, the AOF made an annual contribution towards its upkeep; the contribution for 1865 was a very generous £90.

Details about the start of the lifeboat station are sketchy. Lifeboat historian Jeff Morris has established that *Forester* reached Aberystwyth by train on December 16, 1864, and according to him, would have been sailed down to New Quay that very day, or failing that, the next day December 17, when the station would formally have been 'Opened'. In those days, the Naming Ceremony generally took place within a couple of days of the lifeboat arriving at the station.

Arthur Hood, Chief Officer of the Coastguard, was appointed Hon Sec in 1864, a post he was to hold until 1868 when he was succeeded by another CO of the Coastguard, Mr James Barry. Mr Thomas Evans then took over and was followed by the Rev James Griffiths in 1872 and Mr M Fitzpatrick, CO of the Coastguard. Capt Thomas Jones was Hon Sec from 1875 to 1880 and Capt David James held the post from 1881 until 1890.

Forester was launched for the first time in December 1867. In 1868, The Foresters' Miscellany published the following item: 'Mr James Barry, the Chief Officer of the Coastguard at New Quay station, reports that *Forester* was launched on the evening

A lino print of the lifeboat *Nelson* created by Stuart Evans, of the Ceredigion County Museum, Aberystwyth, based on the 1872 model and created specially for the 150th anniversary of the lifeboat at New Quay. The lifeboat *Forester* came on station at New Quay in 1864, being renamed *Nelson* in 1872.

Courtesy of Ceredigion Museum

of February 19 to the assistance of a schooner *Catherine*, of New Quay, which was observed during a heavy gale about eight miles off in a dismantled state. Before the arrival of the lifeboat the ship's crew had, however, succeeded in beaching her in safety'.

Forester's first effective service was on February 14, 1870, when Mr Barry launched her to go the aid of a barge off New Quay in heavy seas and a fierce gale.

When *Forester* reached the barge, which was carrying a quarter of a ton of railway iron, she was found to be abandoned, but a number of lifeboatmen went on board and managed to manoeuvre the barge back into the harbour. Mr Barry was quoted in The Times as saying that he could not speak too highly of the lifeboat's behaviour in the heavy sea.

In December, 1871, the RNLI decided to send a new lifeboat to Tynemouth No 2 station. The boat was provided out of the funds raised by the Ancient Order of Foresters and she was duly named *Forester*, the name being transferred from New Quay.

The lifeboat at New Quay was re-named *Nelson*, 'being appropriated to a gift of £680 from an anonymous Lady'.

The first service for the *Nelson* was on October 16, 1872, when she was launched at dusk into heavy seas and a NNE gale to aid the *Antigua*, of Greenock, which was at anchor in Cardigan Bay with her main, mizzen and topmasts all shattered.

In the appalling conditions, the *Antigua* could not be found and *Nelson* returned to shore. She put to sea again later with new information on the location of the ship, and found the *Antigua* just before midnight.

The master requested the assistance of a tug, and the lifeboat returned to shore again to pass this message on. She then returned to the *Antigua* to stand by until the tug arrived.

In 1875, EM Lewis was appointed coxswain and the *Nelson's* next major service on New Year's Day, 1880, was to end in controversy. This report is from the Cardigan and Tivyside Advertiser of July 30, 1880: 'On the 1st of January, 1880, the *Nelson* lifeboat put off to the aid of the barque *Pacific* of Swansea which was in a dangerous position in the bay during a fresh westerly gale. One of the lifeboatmen was put on board the vessel, and piloted her out of danger'.

Jeff Morris recounts: 'There was a very unfortunate sequel to this service. Having helped to save this valuable ship and her cargo, Coxswain Lewis and his crew claimed salvage, as they were entitled to do.

'They were awarded £325, but then refused to pay the RNLI the customary two shares for the use of the lifeboat. The matter was eventually resolved, but Coxswain Lewis was dismissed, being succeeded by Owen Evans'.

The *Nelson's* last service was to aid a brigantine in distress off New Quay on November 21, 1884, in a severe north-easterly gale; *Nelson* was launched in heavy seas and located *Albert*, of Carlisle, which had been close to Dublin before being blown off course, subsequently into Cardigan Bay.

Nelson stayed by the brigantine and her crew of five all night, and with the help of the lifeboatmen, the vessel and her crew were brought to safety.

NEW QUAY, 1870.

New Quay harbour 1870, the oldest known photograph of New Quay, showing the new lifeboat station, then only six years old, the single-storey building at the top of the slip on South John Street above the quay. Halfway up Glanmor Terrace in the middle of the picture are the now long-lost clom-built thatched cottages. Looking down on the scene is a man working astride the crosstree on a schooner on the Patent Slip.

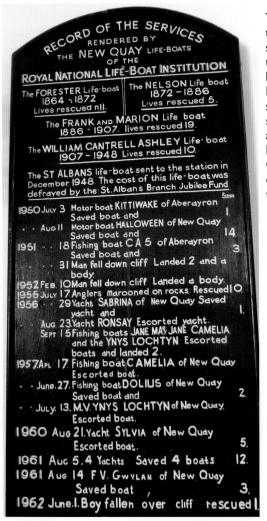

RECORD OF THE SERVICES
RENDERED BY
THE NEW QUAY LIFE-BOATS
OF THE
ROYAL NATIONAL LIFE-BOAT INSTITUTION

The FORESTER Life-boat
1864 – 1872
Lives rescued nil.

The NELSON Life boat
1872 – 1886
Lives rescued 5.

The FRANK AND MARION Life boat
1886 – 1907. lives rescued 19.

The WILLIAM CANTRELL ASHLEY Life-boat
1907 – 1948 Lives rescued 10.

The ST ALBANS life-boat sent to the station in December 1948. The cost of this life-boat was defrayed by the St. Albans Branch Jubilee Fund

1950 JULY 3 Motor boat KITTIWAKE of Aberayron Saved boat and .... 1.
- AUG 11 Motor boat HALLOWEEN of New Quay Saved boat and 14
1951 - 18 Fishing boat C A 5 of Aberayron Saved boat and .... 3.
- 31 Man fell down cliff Landed 2 and a body.
1952 FEB. 10 Man fell down cliff Landed a body.
1955 JULY 17 Anglers marooned on rocks. Rescued 10.
1956 - 29 Yacht SABRINA of New Quay Saved yacht and .... 1.
- AUG 23 Yacht RONSAY Escorted yacht.
SEPT 15 Fishing boats JANE MAY JANE CAMELIA and the YNYS LOCHTYN Escorted boats and landed 2.
1957 APL 17 Fishing boat CAMELIA of New Quay Escorted boat.
- June. 27. Fishing boat DOLIUS of New Quay Saved boat and .... 2.
- JULY 13. M.V. YNYS LOCHTYN of New Quay. Escorted boat.
1960 AUG 21 Yacht SYLVIA of New Quay Escorted boat. .... 5.
1961 AUG 5. 4 Yachts Saved 4 boats .... 12.
1961 AUG 14 F V. GWYLAN of New Quay Saved boat , ... 3.
1962 JUNE.1. Boy fallen over cliff rescued 1.

The earliest board in the lifeboat station showing the Record of the Services Rendered by the New Quay Lifeboats. The first service records are sketchy in detail, but all services undertaken by lifeboats at New Quay are detailed in a comprehensive list at the back of the book.

A special commemorative board for *Nelson* in the lifeboat station. It is inscribed: The cost of the Life Boat NELSON formerly stationed here was presented to the Institution by a Lady in 1872. The board was presented by the RNLI to the station in 1887.

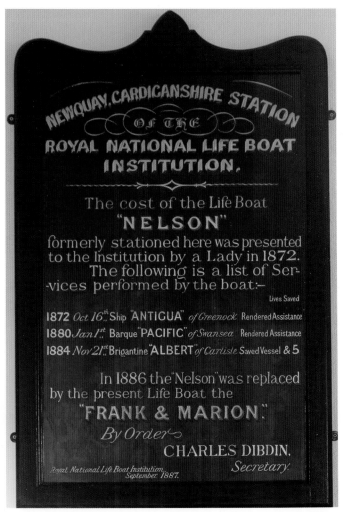

NEWQUAY, CARDIGANSHIRE STATION
OF THE
ROYAL NATIONAL LIFE BOAT
INSTITUTION.

The cost of the Life Boat
"NELSON"
formerly stationed here was presented to the Institution by a Lady in 1872.
The following is a list of Services performed by the boat:—

Lives Saved

1872 Oct 16th. Ship "ANTIGUA" of Greenock Rendered Assistance
1880 Jan 1st. Barque "PACIFIC" of Swansea Rendered Assistance
1884 Nov 21st. Brigantine "ALBERT" of Carlisle Saved Vessel & 5

In 1886 the "Nelson" was replaced by the present Life Boat the
"FRANK & MARION".
By Order
CHARLES DIBDIN,
Secretary.

Royal National Life Boat Institution
September. 1887.

New Quay Harbour List of Tolls and Dues

The New Quay Harbour Act, 1835, stipulated the Tolls and Duties that could be collected for goods landed at the harbour. All foreign vessels were charged 8d a ton if unloading; British ships paid 4d, while New Quay vessels paid 3d. The Third Schedule specified a list of Tolls and Duties to be levied on a large number of goods, both imported and exported.

It was a long list, with some interesting entries alongside more obvious items. The duty on a ton of coal was 4d; every chest of tea one shilling; every ton of salt one and sixpence. The duty on a hundredweight of feathers was two shillings, and on every calf, sheep, pig or fox 4d. Every billiard table was charged five shillings. A corpse incurred a toll of 10 shillings (a coffin covered with velvet also incurred a payment of 10 shillings).

The boards had fallen into a sorry state of repair, but were expertly refurbished in 2013 by Stuart Evans and Stephanie Jameson at Ceredigion Museum, Aberystwyth.

The Aberystwyth Observer,

CARDIGANSHIRE AND MONTGOMERYSHIRE ADVERTISER, AND MERIONETHSHIRE NEWS.

XXIX. No 207·8]   REGISTERED FOR TRANSMISSION ABROAD.   **OCTOBER 2, 1886.**   BY DELIVERY—PREPAID, 6s. 6d.; CREDIT, 7s. 6d.   BY POST— " 8s. 8d., " 10s. 6d.   [PRICE THREE HALF-PENCE.

NEW QUAY.

LAUNCH OF THE NEW LIFE-BOAT.—The celebration of the first launch of the new lifeboat, Frank and Marion, was performed at New Quay on Thursday, Sept. 23rd, the whole town taking a holiday, and the inhabitants as well as those of the district for miles around turning out in honour of the occasion. The new boat, which is the gift of Mr and Mrs Francis J. Smart, of Tunbridge Wells, and is named after them, is built on the same principle as the old one, Nelson, but there are many improvements in matters of detail. It has a series of water-ballast tanks running along amidships, and these are divided into compartments, each having its own plug and pump by which it can be filled or emptied in one minute. There is also an improvement in the rowing crutch and oar, giving the men greater power with less strain on their arms. Mr and Mrs Smart having signified their intention of being present on the occasion, a most enthusiastic reception was given them. A procession was formed near the Lion Hotel, whence it proceeded to the harbour. First came the coastguards, led by their chief officer (Mr Murch); then the life-saving brigade marched; and these were followed by the lifeboat crew, led by the coxswain (Captain Evans). Then came the generous donors, and the rear made up of the members of the lifeboat local committee. In a few minutes the boat was ready for the water, but before the boat was knocked off, the Rev D. Griffith read an address of thanks to Mr and Mrs Smart. Mr Smart, in a few sentences, appropriately acknowledged the receipt of the address, and said that it gave him and his wife great pleasure to be present. They had always taken a great interest in the affairs of the institution, this being the fourth boat presented by them. A short religious service was then conducted by the Rev Mr Griffith, after which the ceremony of christening the boat was performed by Mrs Smart, who broke the customary wine bottle over the stern as the boat glided into the water, amid the vociferous cheering of the crowd. The cheering was renewed when Mr and Mrs Smart, accompanied by several ladies and gentlemen, embarked on board the boat, and took a short trip along the coast. At night the whole place was illuminated, all the houses being lit up by candles and lamps, and as the town is built in terraces on the brow of a hill overlooking the sea, the effect was remarkably pleasing. Tar barrels also blazed forth at several prominent places. On Friday afternoon tea was provided for the lifeboat crew and their wives and for the school children by the generous donors, who were then escorted back to the Lion Hotel.

10

Frank and Marion

THE RNLI sent a new lifeboat to New Quay in 1886, *Frank and Marion*, arriving on station in September. She was 37ft x 8ft, a 12-oared self-righting boat built by Forrestt & Son of Limehouse, London, who were to build 115 lifeboats before the turn of the century. The cost of the boat, £374, was met out of a gift by Dr and Mrs Francis Smart, of Tunbridge Wells, Kent.

Dr Francis Gray Smart (1844-1912) was born at Scarborough, Yorkshire, the son of Dr John Cass Smart. He graduated from Cambridge with an MA and MB in 1870 and carried out medical practice first in Scarborough, then in Tunbridge Wells. Dr Smart was an orthodox physician who later converted to homeopathy, and became a rich man; when he died in 1913, he left estate worth net £445,254.

Among his bequests was £10,000 to his old college Gonville and Caius, Cambridge, for two studentships in his name in natural history or botany – these studentships are still current. In 1886, Dr Smart had married Mrs Marion Pender Jones-Gibb,

widow of Mr Thomas Jones-Gibb, who was rich in her own right. A year earlier, Mrs Jones-Gibb had paid for a new lifeboat at Barmouth, built at a cost of £390. Named the *Jones-Gibb*, the boat was active on station at Barmouth until 1905, and in 1886 Dr Smart and his wife jointly made a gift of a lifeboat to New Quay. When she died in 1913, Mrs Smart, left estate of £750,442 (gross), £698,419 (net).

A public holiday was declared on September 23, 1886, for the Naming Ceremony and Service of Dedication of the new lifeboat and the whole town took part in the celebrations. The Aberystwyth Observer reported that a procession started near the Black Lion Hotel and proceeded down Glanmor Terrace to the harbour. The Chief Coastguard Officer Mr Murch led the way, followed by the life-saving brigade and the lifeboat crew with Coxswain Evans, then the benefactors, Dr Frank and Mrs Marion Smart, and finally members of the lifeboat committee.

Mrs Smart, watched by an extremely large and enthusiastic crowd, named the boat *Frank and Marion* with a bottle of wine over the stern. There was more cheering when Dr and Mrs Smart, accompanied by several ladies and gentlemen, embarked on board the boat for a short trip round the bay. The newspaper report went on : 'At night the whole place was illuminated, all the houses being lit up by candles and lamps, and as the town is built in terraces on the brow of a hill overlooking the sea, the effect was remarkably pleasing'. In the evening, a tea was laid on for 550 people.

The new boat did not have to wait long for her first effective service. On May 20,1887, *Frank and Marion* was launched at 6.30am after a schooner, *Industry*, of Aberystwyth, on her way from Bristol with a general cargo, was driven from her moorings in the harbour by heavy seas in a north-westerly gale.

The crew of the cargo ship dropped anchor in a dangerous position in New Quay Bay, but as the waves battered and swept over the ship, Coxswain Evans managed to manoeuvre the lifeboat alongside and the crew of four was rescued

Winching the lifeboat up and down the steep slope from the lifeboat station to the quay was proving a problem and in 1895, the boathouse was extended at the back by four feet to house the installation of a more powerful winch.

The boat was next called into service, in very heavy seas and a northerly gale, on November 7, 1900. The *Ann Eliza* heading for her home port of Cardigan with ballast was seen drifting towards the shore near New Quay. The Rocket Apparatus team tried to get a line aboard, but the wind changed direction and the dandy began to drift out to sea. *Frank and Marion* was launched at 5am, rescuing two men and a boy. The ship later ran aground on Traethgwyn and was totally wrecked.

Another successful service in a westerly gale and heavy seas was in September, 1903, to assist the ketch *Isabel*, of Milford Haven, which had just discharged her cargo at Cei Bach. She was headed for New Quay when she was caught in a gale and failed to reach the harbour. Drifting dangerously, her sails had been torn off in the storm and the crew dropped both anchors.

The *Frank and Marion* was launched at 1.30am after distress signals from the ketch were seen two miles off New Quay. The boat was located and at the behest of the master, the lifeboat took him, five men on board and his crew of three, to New Quay, landing at 3am. By 6am, the storm had subsided and the lifeboat was launched again with a set of spare sails, which were rigged aboard *Isabel*, and the lifeboat towed the vessel successfully to Aberaeron, arriving exhausted at 11am.

In 1903 work began on a new Boathouse and launchway on a new (and still the present) site next to the Patent Slip along the beach from the harbour and pier. The work was completed in 1904 at a cost of £1,312-5s-10d and the Boathouse was opened by Mrs Catherine Longcroft of Plas Llanina. It has undergone a number of extensions and modifications since then. The old lifeboat house became known as Cnwc-y-Glap, the meeting place for the many master mariners in New Quay to share their memories of life on the ocean wave. It is still in use today.

At the end of 1905, Owen Evans retired after serving as Coxswain for 25 years and was presented with a Certificate of Service by the RNLI in recognition of his years of devoted service. David Davies became the new Coxswain.

Detail from an albumen print by J Price of the Naming Ceremony and Service of Dedication for *Frank and Marion* on September 23, 1886, on the packed pier with everyone in their best clothes. There appear to be only two people afforded the luxury of sitting down for the ceremony – a gentleman with a long beard, wearing a bowler, and a white-haired lady with a dark dress and light overcoat and choker. They are in the centre of the photograph and it cannot be unreasonable to deduce that the couple were the benefactors, Dr Francis and Marion Smart, who we know from the newspaper report were at the ceremony.

The *Frank and Marion* lifeboat after the naming ceremony. According to the newspaper report, the benefactors were taken on a short tour along the coast with other ladies and gentlemen. Frank and Marion can be seen at the far end of the boat, both standing: Frank on the right, next to a lady on his right wearing clothes very similar to the lady in the main picture. Research in Tunbridge Wells has established that Dr Smart did have a long dark beard, and that Marion had distinctive silver-coloured hair.

An uphill struggle: The crew about to rehouse *Frank and Marion* at the end of the Naming Ceremony and Service of Dedication.

New Quay, from the Pier.

A view of New Quay harbour from the pier in the early 1900s. Postcard from the Peter Davis Collection.

Frank and Marion being launched down the slipway on logs used as rollers; this was a difficult and dangerous procedure. Pulling the boat back up the very steep slope was even more difficult. The name *Frank and Marion* can just be made out above the Lifeboat Shield on the bow of the boat. The crew are wearing their cork lifejackets first issued in 1854.

The crew of the New Quay lifeboat lined up in their cork life-jackets in 1899:
Front row (left to right): Name not known, Principality, now Maldwyn; Capt Davies, Araminta; Johnny Evans, Tyllwyd; Dado Thomas; Name not known, Towyn Point; John Elias Thomas; Robert Williams, 5 Rock Street; Capt James, Cranogfa, now Gwynedd; Lewis Davies, Rangel; Capt D Robert Williams, Hafandawel; Johnny Evans, sen; Capt Phillips, Jane and Mary, 10 High Terrace; John Hughes, Mason Square; David Davies, 2 White Street; Owen Evans, Wellington Inn, Coxswain.
Back row (left to right): Capt Evans, Marwood, High Terrace; Thomas Jones, Mason; Thomas Jones's son.

NEW QUAY AUG 05

Frank and Marion ready to go on exercise in New Quay Bay in August, 1905. The white oars on the port side of the lifeboat are clearly visible. The photograph was taken just over a year before her last service – the *Eleander* on November 19, 1906.

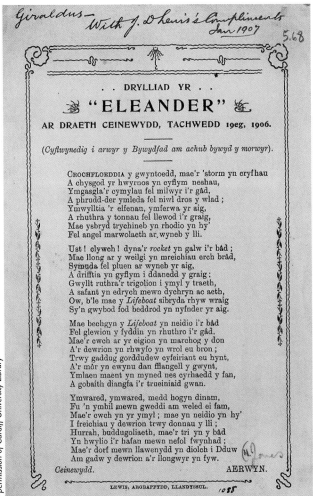

Giraldus — With J. D. Lewis's Compliments Jan 1907 5.68

. . DRYLLIAD YR . .

"ELEANDER"

AR DRAETH CEINEWYDD, TACHWEDD 19eg, 1906.

(Cyflwynedig i arwyr y Bywydfad am achub bywyd y morwyr).

CROCHFLOEDDIA y gwyntoedd, mae'r 'storm yn cryfhau
A chysgod yr hwyrnos yn cyflym neshau,
Ymgasgla'r cymylau fel milwyr i'r gâd,
A phrudd-der ymleda fel niwl dros y wlad;
Ymwylltia 'r elfenau, ymferwa yr aig,
A rhutha y tonnau fel llewod i'r graig,
Mae ysbryd trychineb yn rhodio yn hy'
Fel angel marwolaeth ar wyneb y lli.

Ust! clywch! dyna'r *rocket* yn galw i'r bâd;
Mae llong ar y weilgi yn mreichiau erch brâd,
Symuda fel pluen ar wyneb yr aig,
A drifftia yn gyflym i ddaneddy y graig;
Gwyllt ruthra'r trigolion i ymyl y traeth,
A safant yn edrych mewn dychryn ac aeth,
Ow, b'le mae y *Lifeboat* sibryda rhyw wraig
Sy'n gwybod fod beddrod yn nyfnder yr aig.

Mae bechgyn y *Lifeboat* yn neidio i'r bâd
Fel glewion y fyddin yn rhuthro i'r gâd,
Mae'r cwch ar yr eigion yn marchog y don
A'r dewrion yn rhwyfo yn wrol eu bron;
Trwy gaddug gorddudew cyfeiriant eu hynt,
A'r môr yn ewynu dan fflangell y gwynt,
Ymlaen maent yn myned nes cyrhaedd y fan,
A gobaith diangfa i'r trueiniaid gwan.

Ymwared, ymwared, medd hogyn dinam,
Fu 'n ymbil mewn gweddi am weled ei fam,
Mae'r cwch yn yr ymyl; mae yn neidio yn hy'
I freichiau y dewrion trwy donnau y lli;
Hurrah, buddugoliaeth, mae'r tri yn y bâd
Yn hwylio i'r hafan mewn nefol fwynhad;
Mae'r dorf mewn llawenydd yn diolch i Dduw
Am gadw y dewrion a'r llongwyr yn fyw.

Ceinewydd.   AERWYN.

LEWIS, ARGRAFFYDD, LLANDYSSUL. 1055

Frank and Marion's last two services were on the same day – November 19, 1906. At 7.45am, the lifeboat was launched in a gale when the schooner *Two Brothers*, of Porthmadog, homeward bound from Waterford, was spotted flying a distress signal in heavy seas. *Frank and Marion* helped to bring the schooner safely into the harbour and the lifeboat was then re-housed.

Less than than 12 hours after the first launch, *Frank and Marion* was called into action again after a ketch, *Leander,* of Caernarfon, was in trouble in New Quay Bay. The lifeboatmen rescued the crew of three and landed back at New Quay at 8pm. This second service of the day for the *Frank and Marion* in a northerly gale and very heavy seas proved to be her last.

The last rescue was celebrated in a Welsh ballad that was written at the time:

. . SHIPWRECK OF THE . .

"ELEANDER"

on New Quay Beach, November 19th, 1906.
(Presented to the heroes of the Lifeboat for saving the lives of the sailors).

This poem by Aerwyn (H Jones) was published by Lewis of Llandyssul soon after the event. Here the boat is the *Eleander*, but clearly the poem which tells of the rescue of the three crew members describes the *Leander* incident. JD Lewis, the founder of Gomer Press, inscribed the poem in January, 1907. More than 100 years later, Gomer Press were to print this book.

William Cantrell Ashley

A NEW lifeboat arrived at New Quay in 1907 that would prove to be the longest-serving lifeboat at the Station. She was 35ft x 10ft, a non-self-righting boat built by Thames Ironworks at a cost of £961. Named *William Cantrell Ashley*, she was provided out of a legacy in the will of Charles Carr Ashley, of Mentone, in the south of France, late of Kingston-upon-Thames, Surrey, who died aged 65 in 1906 leaving estate of £80,486 net.

After giving £1,000 to Battersea Dogs' Home, and along with a small number of private bequests, he left the remainder (which amounted to around £70,000) to the RNLI to form an Ashley Lifeboat Fund.

The terms of the bequest were strict and the conditions, as reported in The Times, were quite clear – the fund was to be applied as follows:

1) Within 12 months of his death, to provide and equip five first class lifeboats (not steam) to be called the Susan Ashley, Charles Henry Ashley, Richard Ashley, William Cantrell Ashley, and Fifi and Charles, with the necessary houses, carriages, &c., to be stationed as such points on the English and Welsh coasts as the committee may determine, preference being given to the south coast . . .

2) To set apart a fund to provide in perpetuity for the maintenance and upkeep of the said five boats, &c., including an annual allowance for depreciation or replacements and as and when necessary to replace such boats by others with such further improvements, &c., as may seem desirable, provided that such renewals shall bear the name of such one of the five boats, &c., as they shall replace.

3) The balance of the fund to be applied for the benefit of the widows and families of lifeboatmen who have lost their lives in endeavouring to save life at sea, preference being given to any of the crews of the said five lifeboats.

4) The stations of the various lifeboats may be altered from time to time as exigencies of lifeboat work shall determine.

This was a Take It or Leave It offer. The Times reported that if the RNLI did not accept the bequest on the above conditions, 'The testator left the whole of his residuary estate to the Hospital for Diseases of the Chest at Brompton, to build and endow at the Isle of Wight establishment, a Susan Ashley wing or ward in memory of his late mother, Susan Ashley'.

The RNLI quickly agreed to the terms, and the five lifeboats stipulated in the bequest were established in 1906 and 1907. One was *William Cantrell Ashley*, which was taken by rail from London to Fishguard in October, 1907, and then sailed on to New Quay by the same crew of 15 men who had taken the previous lifeboat *Frank and Marion* to Fishguard on her last voyage ready to be taken to the RNLI depot in London. Only two of the 15 crew – Tom Elias Thomas and David Evans, Awelfryn – were still alive when the *William Cantrell Ashley* was retired in 1948.

After effective services in 1915 and 1916, the *William Cantrell Ashley* was called out at 9am on August 22, 1917, to rescue two boys who had gone out in a small fishing boat when the weather deteriorated and a southerly gale developed. Rowing back towards New Quay harbour, a local fishing boat *Daniel and Jane* was spotted in difficulties with the sails badly damaged. Coxswain Davies changed course and discovered that the disabled boat was half-full of water. The crew of two was rescued and were landed with the two boys at New Quay.

William Cantrell Ashley was called out to assist an altogether bigger vessel in November 1920. HMS *Amethyst*, a Royal Navy Topaze-class cruiser and veteran of the Dardanelles campaign and the Gallipoli landings in 1915, had been sold as scrap after the war and was being towed south by two tugs to Milford Haven when they ran into a gale and very heavy seas.

The towline broke and *William Cantrell Ashley* answered the call for help; when it arrived on the scene, the crew must have feared the worst. *Amethyst* displaced 3,000 tons and was 360ft long compared with the 35ft long lifeboat, effectively not much more than a wooden rowing boat. Undeterred, the lifeboatmen managed to get the seven crew aboard and brought them ashore. The captain refused to leave and was rescued by the Aberystwyth lifeboat two days later as the storm raged on.

There were some personnel changes at this time. David Davies had been the Coxswain from 1905 until 1918; he was succeeded by Frederick Shaylor who held the position until 1935; David Evans took over to be followed in 1936 by James Garfield Williams. In February 1937, Capt David Rees died aged 89, after serving as Hon Sec for 47 years, an extraordinary achievement. He was awarded inscribed binoculars in 1901 and an inscribed barometer in 1933 in recognition of his service to the RNLI. He was succeeded as Hon Sec by his son, Mr D Brinley Rees.

The crew of the *William Cantrell Ashley* was involved in an exhausting 14-hour service in 1930. The lifeboat was launched at 1pm on March 20 'in the presence of a large crowd' according to the Tivyside Gazette, to go to the assistance of a local fishing boat *Rose* with two men on board.

In a full westerly gale and very rough seas, the *Rose* headed north towards Aberystwyth closely followed by the lifeboat. Despite losing her mainsail in the storm, the fishing boat managed to drop anchor and the crew of two boarded a local boat and landed at Aberystwyth harbour, 'where thousands of people had assembled to watch their arrival'.

William Cantrell Ashley being rehoused in the new lifeboat station. The wheels had been fitted with Tipping's Plates, which consisted of seven iron plates bolted round the large rear wheels of the carriage. As the wheel turned, two plates were always beneath the wheel (rather like early caterpillar tracks) to prevent the carriage sinking into soft sand.

Launching the Lifeboat more than one hundred years ago: a pre-First World War postcard by DO Jones & Son showing the *William Cantrell Ashley* being launched from the new boathouse, with the long-lost poles of Penpolion in the background. The Jones family had a photographic studio in Park Street, New Quay, from the late 1890s until 1930.

William Cantrell Ashley on her carriage in the new lifeboat house in 1908, four years after it opened and one year after coming on station. The sign above the door says National Lifeboat Institute LIFE BOAT Supported by Voluntary Contributions. On one door is the first Record of Service board. Postcard from the Peter Davis Collection.

Having established that the fishermen were safe, the crew of the lifeboat then headed back to New Quay, battling their way in the dark against a very strong wind through very heavy seas. The lifeboat was under the command of Second Coxswain Thomas Thomas and did not reach the station until 3am on March 21. Some of the crew were exhausted and needed medical attention.

When a local fishing boat *Peggy* was reported overdue on May 31, 1938, the lifeboat was launched at 1.45pm and was soon joined in the search by the motor lifeboat from Aberystwyth, *Frederick Angus*. It would be another ten years before New Quay had a motor lifeboat on station, but it was the 12-oared *William Cantrell Ashley* that found *Peggy* at 4pm six miles north-east of New Quay Head and escorted her back to harbour at 5.10pm. The motor lifeboat was recalled to Aberystwyth.

One of the last services the *William Cantrell Ashley* undertook involved another Royal Navy vessel on its way to Milford Haven and the breaker's yard. HMS *Universal*, a U-class submarine, broke down in very rough seas nine miles west of South Bishop Lighthouse and a Royal Navy destroyer took the stricken submarine in tow. The towline broke and the submarine drifted north in Cardigan Bay.

The lights of the submarine and the destroyer were visible from New Quay and the lifeboat was launched at 6.20am; she was standing by the two naval vessels when the Fishguard lifeboat returned to the scene at 8.50am, later to be joined by the Aberystwyth lifeboat. The New Quay lifeboat left the scene at 11am, returning to the boathouse at 2.30pm. All attempts to take the submarine in tow failed, and 16 crew were rescued by the Fishguard Lifeboat, and 11 by the Aberystwyth boat.

This was to prove almost the last service for the *William Cantrell Ashley*. She had served at New Quay for 41 years from 1907 to 1948 and was the RNLI's last pulling and sailing boat in station service; her departure and the arrival at New Quay of *St Albans* meant that the RNLI's fleet was now totally motorised.

When *William Cantrell Ashley* sailed out to meet the new lifeboat in New Quay Bay in December 1948, the scene was captured by a BBC TV film crew – according to Edward Wake-Walker, former Public Relations Director of the RNLI, this was the first time an RNLI lifeboat had ever appeared on television.

The RNLI presented the *William Cantrell Ashley* to the Outward Bound School at Aberdovey to where she was sailed by some of her old crew and members of the Station Committee.

Having been in the hands of a number of private owners, *William Cantrell Ashley* is now in the care of Amgueddfa Cymru/National Museum Wales at their Collections Centre at Nantgarw near Cardiff. The boat is unrestored but in sound condition.

When the original five lifeboats from the 1906 Ashley bequest were retired, the legacy paid for another five boats, and their names were passed on to the new boats.

The *William Cantrell Ashley* name was given to a Liverpool Class motor lifeboat built in 1949, which served at Clovelly, Devon, for many years. Eventually this boat was restored by the Hoylake Lifeboat Museum and is now moored in Albert Dock, Liverpool, where the public can view her and sail in her.

William Cantrell Ashley at sea in full sail and with a full complement of 15 crew, comprising coxswain, assistant coxswain, bowman and 12 oarsmen. The sails would have been coloured red in the 1920s and 1930s.

JUST A LINE FROM NEW QUAY

GOOD LUCK

Launched upon the foaming wave,
Comes the lifeboat forth to save ;
While in behind she brings to you
Many an interesting view.

1249

Peter Davis Collection

Left: a Novelty Postcard from the 1930s. A flap (just discernible in the card) lifts up to reveal a concertina of 12 small photo-views of New Quay.

Above: an early photo of the Boathouse with *William Cantrell Ashley* on station and Glanmor Terrace in the background.

The *William Cantrell Ashley* showing off her lines as she is beached near the quay in front of the Harbour Warehouse. The harbour toll boards are clearly visible; the buildings later became the yacht club.

NEW QUAY LIFEBOAT CREW, MARCH 1937.

The crew in their oilskins, March 1937: *Back row (left to right):* Capt Ivor Williams, Daniel Owen Davies, Dai Fred Davies, Meurig Lewis, Phil Jones, Argo James, Jack Evans, David Enoc Davies. *Middle row (left to right):* Evan Evans, David Richards, Fred Shaylor, Jim Jones, Glanmor Rees. *Front row (left to right):* Timothy Thomas, James Garfield Williams (coxswain), Arden Evans (second coxswain).

William Cantrell Ashley preparing to leave New Quay for the last time in February 1949 after 41 years of service. It was an historic day as she was the RNLI's last pulling and sailing boat on station service and the crew were sorry to see her go. 'She is as good a boat as any,' one of the lifeboat crew was quoted in the Cambrian News.

A Television First in New Quay Bay: The motorised lifeboat *St Albans* enters the harbour with Coxswain Arden Evans at the wheel on December 12, 1948, after a torrid passage of 410 miles from Cowes, to be greeted by *William Cantrell Ashley* in full sail. The RNLI fleet was now completely motorised, and a BBC TV film crew was on hand to capture the moment – the first time a lifeboat had ever been seen on television.

St Albans

THE NEW lifeboat was *St Albans*, the first motorised boat at New Quay. Built at the Groves and Gutteridge yard at Cowes on the Isle of Wight, she was a 35ft 6in x 10ft 8in Liverpool Class non-self-righting boat; two 18hp Weyburn engines gave her a top speed of 7.5 knots. She was provided out of a fund raised in St Albans in 1945 to mark the Silver Jubilee of the city's branch of the RNLI and the *St Albans* was to save more lives than any other New Quay lifeboat before and since.

I am indebted to Brian Doble and Margaret Sharp of the St Albans branch of the RNLI for their research used in this chapter.

The St Albans and District branch of the RNLI had been established in 1920. Miss Lucy Harriet Silvester was the driving force, an extremely well-connected lady, as can be seen by supporters who attended a meeting of the branch in 1921: Lord Salisbury, chairman, and Viscount Curzon, Sir Godfrey Baring, Lt Col AB Murray (district organiser, London) and the Mayor of St Albans. Both Lord Salisbury and Viscount Curzon made speeches appealing for support, Lord Salisbury noting that a Ladies Guild had recently been established nationally 'recognising the talent of the ladies for fundraising'.

Fundraising began on a modest scale, but more than £1,000 was collected in 1941, the branch's 21st year, and at the AGM in 1944, it was reported that a total of £8,000 had been raised since the inception of the branch.

The first mention of funding for a lifeboat to commemorate the Branch's Silver Jubilee in 1945 was noted in the minutes of the AGM: 'It has been decided that it would be a fine gesture to mark the Silver Jubilee of the branch by presenting the Institution with a lifeboat. It would cost £5,000'. Miss Silvester, who was Hon Sec for more than 25 years, described the project as her 'last big effort'. She died in 1956 aged 93.

In 1946, Mr J Terry, HQ organizer for the area, paid tribute to the St Albans branch, which he said was an example to all other branches throughout the country and a riposte to those who say it must be very difficult to interest people in inland places to support the lifeboat.

By 1947, the branch was able to hand the RNLI £5,000 for a

new lifeboat, and construction was well under way in 1948, the final cost of the boat being £9,836. The RNLI provided a tractor, T39, for launching and recovering the boat; a Tractor House was built at a cost of £600 and alterations to the boathouse cost £2,200.

St Albans was sailed the 410 miles from Cowes to New Quay in terrible conditions that proved a severe and real test for the new lifeboat. Dense fog delayed her departure in late November 1948, and the lifeboat was buffeted by strong south-westerly gales, having to put in to several places on the way.

Commander EW Middleton, Western District Inspector of Lifeboats, was in charge and was interviewed by The Hertfordshire Advertiser at the end of the journey.

Cmdr Middleton said that in the channel off the Eddystone Lighthouse, the wind freshened considerably and there was a very bad swell running with nasty sea.

'The appearance of the sky was such that had we been in tropical water, we might have been running into a hurricane or a typhoon'. There was a 90mph wind, and the *St Albans* put into Fowey.

'When approaching the Longships we had a word with the Sennen Cove lifeboat, and they seemed rather surprised that we were attempting to go through the channel in such weather conditions. Off Padstow we encountered another gale of great force with a very heavy breaking sea'.

But *St Albans* overcame the challenges. Cmdr Middleton said, 'She stood up to the very unfavourable conditions wonderfully

well. Her engines worked with absolute smoothness. It was quite incredible to me that we shipped no water to speak of, because there was no doubt from what we saw, that bigger ships were having a very bad time, while we were floating over the water very comfortably'.

He had not, he said, ever met a better crew: Coxswain Arden Evans, Mechanic Gwilym Davies and lifeboatmen Eric Swan and Meurig Lewis. District engineer Mr Ireland was in charge of the machinery.

When news reached New Quay on Sunday, December 12, 1948, that the new lifeboat was approaching, the newspaper reported that 'soon there were sounds of many people scurrying down the steeply sloping streets to the seafront, and flags were hurriedly put out of the windows . . .

'When the *St Albans* finally hove in sight a considerable crowd had assembled as Cmdr Middleton brought her inshore; she was accorded a cordial welcome, in which the crew of the old lifeboat moored at the quay, fully manned and with sails set, took part'.

The boat was welcomed to New Quay the next morning in the Lifeboat Station. Mr Walter Cherry, chairman of the urban council, thanked the RNLI and the people of St Albans for their generosity; Lt-Col Vivian M Lewis, RNLI organising secretary for Wales, thanked the townspeople of New Quay for the splendid welcome.

Finally, Mr Alastair Graham, president of the New Quay branch, added his thanks to the people of St Albans for their 'wonderful gift'.

St Albans in all her majesty and glory in a rare colour photograph. The *St Albans* was the first motorised lifeboat at New Quay and it is thought that this picture was taken on the Solent in 1948 when the boat was on exercise before going on station. She had a torrid time on the 410-mile passage from Cowes to New Quay.

The flags were out and the crowds flocked to the Naming Ceremony and Service of Dedication for the *St Albans* in June 1949. The pier afforded a good viewing spot to enjoy the celebrations, and by the look of it, the sun. A group of Sea Scouts from Aberystwyth was on hand to give assistance.

Members of the crew aboard the *St Albans*. Meurig Lewis, a member of the Dylan Thomas set when the poet lived in New Quay, is in the foreground near the loud-hailer; David John is the next crew member. The tall man at the back of the boat is Norman London House – his claim to fame was that it was said he was the model for Nogood Boyo in Under Milk Wood. Coxswain Arden Evans and Mechanic Gwilym Davies are just about identifiable, wearing white caps.

The Naming and
Dedication service
was on June 25,
1949, and Miss Lucy
Silvester, deputy
chairman of the St
Albans branch of
the RNLI, formally
named the boat
after which she
was presented with
a bouquet by Susan
Jones, Bronwylfa,
who later became the
respected local and
maritime historian
Sue Passmore.

Dignitaries at the naming ceremony: Miss Lucy Silvester is sitting in the front row holding a bouquet next to the Archbishop of Wales, the Most Rev DL Prosser. Mr Alastair Graham, president of the New Quay branch of the RNLI, is third from right in the back row.

The cover of the programme for the Naming Ceremony of *St Albans* on June 25, 1949

The Cambrian News reported that hundreds thronged the pier and foreshore to watch the Naming Ceremony and Service of Dedication on June 25, 1949. The service was conducted by the Archbishop of Wales, the Most Rev DL Prosser. Miss Lucy Silvester, now 85 years old and deputy chairman of the St Albans branch of the RNLI, formally named the boat after which she was presented with a bouquet by Susan Jones. The chairman of the urban district council, Mr Eifion Price, thanked everyone, especially the citizens of St Albans for the gift of the boat. The boat was received on behalf of the New Quay branch by Mr Alstair Graham, president, who again thanked the people of St Albans for 'such a munificent gift'.

A poem – To The Lifeboat St Albans – was specially written for the event by Miss Dorothy M Evans, Montrose, one verse of which went:

Good people of St Albans, you no nobler gift could send,
For there the first of English martyrs died for Him, his friend;
With grateful hearts we thank you, and when she her task fulfills,
Perchance we'll hear your Abbey bells resound o'er Cymric hills.

It was to be a year before *St Albans* was launched on service for the first time. On July 3, 1950, a motor boat had been sighted in rough seas six miles north east of New Quay flying a distress signal. When *St Albans* located the *Kittiwake*, one man was found on board; he had been fishing, but the engine had failed The man was rescued and the boat towed back to New Quay.

A peaceful view of the Lifeboat station in the late 1960s with *St Albans* just visible through the open door. Built in 1904, the station was extended in 1948 when the *St Albans* came on station, and was to undergo further improvements and extensions in later years. Postcard from the Peter Davis collection.

ROYAL NATIONAL LIFE-BOAT INSTITUTION
(Supported entirely by Voluntary Contributions)

NEW QUAY (CARDS.) BRANCH

COMMEMORATION
of the
CENTENARY OF THE LIFE-BOAT STATION
1864 - 1964

on
THE PIER, NEW QUAY
on
FRIDAY, 3rd JULY, 1964, at 2.30 p.m.

The Service will be conducted by
The Right Reverend the Lord Bishop of St. David's

The programme for the Centenary of the Lifeboat Station in 1964 with *St Albans* on the cover.

The Coastguard reported that a motorboat was burning flares two miles off New Quay on August 11, 1950. Fifteen minutes later, the *St Albans* had been launched into very rough seas and a near gale force wind. The lifeboat located the motorboat – *Halloween* – at 5.20pm and discovered there was a crew of two and 12 passengers on board. The engine had broken down, and *St Albans* towed the boat and her 14 occupants into New Quay Harbour at 7.10pm.

Both the New Quay and Aberystwyth lifeboats were launched on January 9, 1952, after the tanker, *Audacity*, of London, was reported to be in difficulties in heavy seas 17 miles north-west of New Quay Head. In a north-westerly gale, the *St Albans* put to sea at 7.50pm, returning to the station at 4.30am, the tanker having been taken in tow by the MV *Alacrity*.

Mr Brinley Rees retired in 1954 after 17 years as Honorary Secretary and was awarded the RNLI's Thanks on Vellum in recognition of his years of service. He was succeeded by Capt J Byron Jones, OBE.

In the afternoon of July 17, 1955, Coxswain Evans informed Capt Jones that ten people had been marooned by the incoming tide on rocks near Birds' Rock. The lifeboat was launched at 4.50pm, taking a small boat with her. Fortunately the sea was calm, and the small boat managed to rescue the ten people, who turned out to be members of an angling club, and ferried them to the *St Albans*, which landed back at New Quay at 5.40pm.

A number of local fishing boats were caught at sea in a sudden south-easterly gale on September 15, 1956. The *St Albans* was launched in very heavy seas and went to the aid of two of the boats, the *Camelia* and *Ynys Lochtyn,* anchored in the lee of Llanina Point waiting for the tide to turn. There were two women passengers aboard the *Ynys Lochtyn,* and the lifeboat went alongside the fishing boat to take the two women on board.

The afternoon of August 5, 1961, turned out to be one of the busiest in the history of the station. *St Albans* was launched at 3.23pm after a woman reported that her husband, who was out in a speedboat, was three hours overdue. In a rough sea and a strong south-westerly wind, the lifeboatmen soon found the missing speedboat, which had been beached safely near Llanina Point. They then went to the assistance of two yachts– each with a crew of three – capsized off Llanina Reef; the yachts were righted and with their crews, taken back to the harbour.

Once there, another boat was seen to be flying a distress signal, and *St Albans* put out to sea again immediately. This boat managed to get back to the harbour under her own power, so the lifeboat moved on to go to the aid of another two yachts which had capsized. The yachts with a total of six people on board were towed back to New Quay, the lifeboatmen eventually returning to the boathouse at 5.30pm.

Gwilym Davies died in 1965 having served the New Quay Lifeboat for 29 years, the last 17 as Motor Mechanic. He was succeeded by Sydney Fowler.

A fine portrait of Arden Evans, Coxswain of the New Quay lifeboat for 11 years from 1947 until his death in 1958. His sons Winston and Idris gave outstanding service to the RNLI.

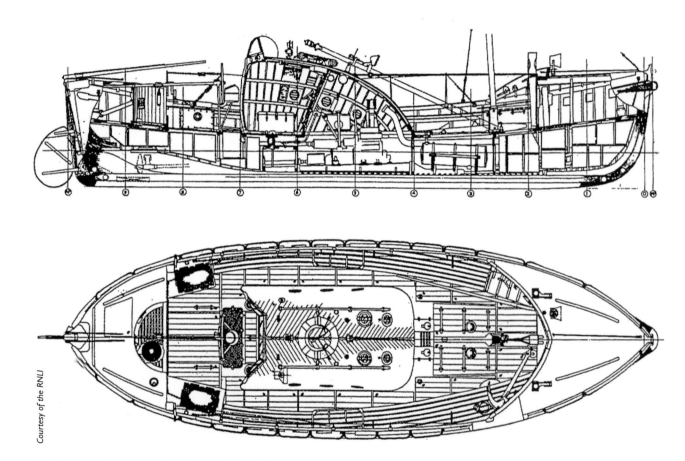

Courtesy of the RNLI

Technical drawings of the 35'6" x 10'8" twin-engined Liverpool Class lifeboat, used by the RNLI from the 1930s until the 1980s. They were orginally single-screw boats; the more powerful twin-screw boats like the *St Albans* were first introduced in 1945 and proved both popular and successful.

An atmospheric picture of *St Albans* on the open water; it is not known when or where it was taken or whether it is being crewed by New Quay men. The Liverpool Class lifeboat was launched 66 times and saved more lives – 78 – in its 21 years on station than any other lifeboat at New Quay before and since.

Three medals awarded after outstanding

Three New Quay lifeboat men were awarded the RNLI's Bronze Medal, two for 'outstanding gallantry' and one for 'skill, courage and fine leadership' after an outstanding rescue on August 7, 1966.

The Hon Sec Capt Byron Jones received a call from the Coastguard at 11.30pm informing him that some boys were missing on the cliffs or the beach in the Llwyncelyn area.

The Coastguard Cliff Rescue Team was activated and Capt Jones alerted Coxswain Winston Evans and Mechanic Sydney Fowler, who went to the station in case the lifeboat was needed.

It was, and *St Albans* was launched at 12.40am to search the beach and cliffs around Gilfach-yr-Halen using her searchlight. Half an hour after arriving at Gilfach-yr-Halen, at around 1.40am, they heard shouts and in the beam of the searchlight they saw a boy stranded on a ledge 20 feet up the cliff.

Coxswain Evans dared not take the lifeboat too close in-shore because of the treacherous waters and submerged rocks. Mechanic Fowler and David Rees, a police sergeant and son of the former Hon Sec Mr DB Rees, who happened to be in New Quay at the time, volunteered to be a member of the crew when the maroons went off, both volunteered to swim ashore.

Coxswain Evans anchored the lifeboat as close to the cliffs as he could and the two men jumped overboard, taking a nylon line with them in case a breeches-buoy was needed.

Both men were strong swimmers but they had difficulty in reaching the foot of the cliffs. They eventually made it and Sgt Rees was able to pull himself up onto the ledge where the boy told them that his two friends had fallen down the cliffs.

The boy, who was 16, was terrified and refused to move. 'A considerable amount of persuasion was needed' before the boy was moved off the ledge and hauled onto the lifeboat where he was treated for exposure and shock.

cliff rescue at Gilfach-yr-Halen

The two lifeboat men were joined by two members of the Coastguard Cliff Rescue Team in their search for the other two boys, who were found on a nearby beach. One was dead, the other seriously injured.

The injured boy was strapped to the Coastguards stretcher but was in too severe a condition to be hauled up the cliff. It was then that Coxswain Evans brought the *St Albans* on to a small beach, Fowler and Rees wading out into the waves to guide the boat in. According to Coxswain Evans, the unsung hero of the operation was coastguard Gerald Lewis, who played a major part in the rescue.

'With great difficulty,' Coxswain Evans held the lifeboat in position 'using his engines and rudder most skilfully'. The injured boy and his dead companion were put aboard, and then the rescuers clambered aboard too.

Both Sydney Fowler and Sgt Rees were suffering from hypothermia, as they had taken off their oilskins before swimming ashore, and were both treated for exposure.

The lifeboat headed back to New Quay at full speed, and it was requested that a doctor and ambulance meet the boat. It was approaching low-tide, so the Hon Sec arranged for a local motor-boat with a doctor and nurse on board to meet the lifeboat. At 2.30am, the injured boy was transferred to the motor-boat, but he died before reaching the shore. The lifeboat was eventually rehoused at 11.10am.

For their 'outstanding gallantry', Sydney Fowler and David Rees were each awarded the Bronze Medal. For his 'great skill, courage and fine leadership', Coxswain Evans was also awarded the Bronze Medal.

They were presented with their medals by Princess Marina, Duchess of Kent, the president of the RNLI, at the annual general meeting in London in March, 1967.

Medal Service Certificates were presented to the other members of the crew – Idris Evans, Picton Williams, Tom Jones, David Davies and Clive Davies.

A photograph taken aboard *St Albans* in September, 1965, when Winston Evans took over as coxswain at 26 years of age, the youngest ever in Britain at that time. From left: Winston Evans, Idris Evans (his brother), Rhoslan Davies, the retiring coxswain at the wheel, and an unnamed Inspector of Lifeboats. Idris became second coxswain aged 21.

Prince Charles dropped in to New Quay after his Investiture as Prince of Wales at Caernarfon Castle in 1969. He came by helicopter landing in Llanina Field, known ever since as Charlie's Field. The Prince met the lifeboat team outside the Cliffside: Winston Evans has got the Prince interested in something or other. Looking on are the Hon Sec, Capt Byron Jones, and behind him (left in the picture), the RNLI branch president Alastair Graham. Members of the lifeboat crew line up behind Winston.

The Inshore Lifeboats

TOWARDS the end of the 1950s, the RNLI was beginning to find that its fleet of lifeboats was not entirely appropriate for dealing with fast-moving incidents happening close to shore. In 1963, the RNLI placed ten high-speed 16ft inflatable rescue boats around the UK for response to these fast-developing incidents. They were 4.95m, 15'6" long, built of neoprene-covered nylon and powered by a 40hp outboard engine, giving the boat a top speed of more than 20 knots and a range of 60 miles.

Today, they are equipped with VHF radio, GPS, night vision equipment, flexible fuel tanks and a spare propeller as well as First Aid kits which include oxygen.

They were ideal for incidents close to the shore involving small boats, as well as rescuing children and bathers and people cut off by the tide where speed, both of response and over the water, is essential; a crew of only two or three was required and the small boats could be launched in minutes. These small inflatable lifeboats quickly proved themselves an essential complement to the all-weather fleet.

D-122, the first inshore lifeboat at New Quay, which came on station in 1967 and soon proved its worth

More development was being undertaken in the late 60s and early 70s by Rear Admiral Desmond Hoare, headmaster of Atlantic College, at St Donats, South Glamorgan. He developed a rigid hull version of an inflatable rescue boat and the RNLI swiftly adopted the principle with its first 21ft Atlantic 21 inshore lifeboat, which entered service in 1972. Very quickly, the D Class inshore rescue boat and the rigid inflatable Atlantic 21 became the two busiest types of lifeboat and their present day successors, not much changed, are still the workhorses of the RNLI fleet.

The first IRB at New Quay was *D-122*, which was commissioned at the station in May 1967. The first effective service was on June 28, 1967. A speedboat *Blue Star* had been reported overdue, and the *St Albans* was launched around 1.00am and, with a number of local fishing boats, searched an area north of Aberporth. At 5.50am it was reported that a sighting had been made three miles north of New Quay Head. The new IRB was launched at 6.09am and found the speedboat floating vertically with just 2 feet of the bows visible above the water.

D-238, the second inshore boat with (from left) crewmen Bunny Evans, Morlais Davies and Mervyn Thomas in Aberaeron Harbour.

The *St Albans* was called and the speedboat recovered and landed back at New Quay at 9.30am. After refuelling, the lifeboat put to sea again to look for the missing person; the body was eventually found and recovered, being landed at New Quay at 2.30pm.

The next service by the *D-122*, on August 12, 1967, proved to be an outstanding one (see next page) and the awards made later to Idris Evans, Trevor Evans and Peter Evans were well deserved. As was the praise from Princess Marina at the RNLI Annual Meeting the following year.

Speed was a key feature of the new ILB as was demonstrated when *D-122* was called out on September 1, 1969. Three minutes after the station was told that a yacht had capsized off Coybal Beach, *D-122* was launched at 4.25pm and soon found the overturned yacht – *Birdchimmer* – with her crew of three in the water. They were rescued and landed on a nearby beach before the ILB returned to the yacht and then back to New Quay arriving at 5.40pm.

Six D-class inshore lifeboats have served at New Quay since 1967: *D-122*, *D-238*, *D-339*, *D-476 Corydd*, *D-616 Amy Lea* and *D-754 Audrey LJ*. Along with the relief ILBs, they have been launched a total of 545 times, with 530 people rescued (including lives saved).

Royal praise for rescue at Cwmtydu

The first inshore lifeboat arrived on station in March 1967 and it was not long before she took part in an outstanding service with a three-man crew whose average age was 19.

At 5pm on August 12, the Hon Sec Capt Byron Jones contacted coxswain Winston Evans to say that two holidaymakers were in difficulties off Cwmtydu three miles south of New Quay and were being swept out to sea.

Coxswain Evans fired off the maroons calling out both lifeboat crews. The weather was bad – the sea was rough with a Force 7 northwesterly, gusting Force 8.

Because speed was essential, Capt Jones decided to send the inshore lifeboat *D-122*, which would be backed up by the *St Albans*. *D-122* was launched at 5.08pm with Idris Evans, the lifeboat's second coxswain, at the helm. The 23-year-old had two teenagers as crew – Trevor Evans and Peter Evans.

The sea became very rough when the boat rounded New Quay Head – Trevor Evans remembers the boat being hurled vertical in very rough water near Birds' Rock. They reached Cwmtydu at 5.20pm and people on the cliffs directed the lifeboat to two people in the water, only yards from the cliff face and in very heavy and 'confused' water caused by the heavy backwash from the cliffs.

The first bather they found was a woman. She was wearing a lifebelt, and a line was thrown to her but she was very weak and hardly had enough strength to hold it. In a dangerous manoeuvre, helmsman Evans took the IRB into the worst of the water at the base of the cliffs. The woman was hauled aboard and the two 17-year-old crewmen began mouth-to-mouth resuscitation. The boat then went towards the second bather, the woman's husband, but he was found to be dead when he was picked up.

Conditions continued to deteriorate which meant that the boat could not land at Cwmtydu. With the crewmen continuing to give the kiss-of-life to the woman, Helmsman Evans headed back to New Quay. They met up with the *St Albans* but the weather was so bad the inshore lifeboat could not get alongside; blankets were passed from the St Albans to *D-122* for the woman and the crew, and a doctor and ambulance were requested to meet the lifeboat at New Quay Harbour. The lifeboat reached New Quay at 5.40pm, and the woman was taken to hospital, where happily she made a full recovery.

For this excellent service, helmsman Idris Evans and crewmen Trevor Evans and Peter Evans were each awarded the RNLI's Thanks on Vellum.

Idris Evans is presented with the RNLI's Thanks on Vellum for his role in the Cwmtydu rescue. His 17-year-old crewmen Peter Evans and Trevor Evans look on, with Alastair Graham, (right), president of the New Quay branch of the RNLI, and Idris's daughter Joanne.

The rescued woman, Mrs Mavis Moon of Bristol, later wrote to the crew: 'I shall never forget that you risked your lives to recover my husband's body, and myself.

'And that but for your efforts, my children would now be without father *and* mother. From the bottom of my heart, I thank you for your bravery. I shall never forget your courageous act'.

This was followed by Royal praise for the crew when Princess Marina referred to the rescue in her presidential address at the Annual meeting of the RNLI in London in 1968:

'One of the most impressive facts in the annual report is the remarkable development of a relatively new arm of the lifeboat service, that of the inshore rescue boats. Because of the characteristics of the boats, their crews tend on the whole to be fairly young men.

'Indeed in one of the outstanding inshore rescue boat services last year, carried out at New Quay in Cardiganshire, two of the three members of the crew were aged 18.'

In fact, Trevor and Peter Evans were even younger, both aged 17 at the time of the rescue.

They had turned 18 when they received their awards.

53

THE Cardigan Bay Regatta at New Quay held in August has a long and proud history. It was first held in 1875, although there were unofficial rowing races between local fishermen and coastguards as far back as 1835. The highlight is the annual yacht race from North Wales to New Quay. The race, which has been called Wales's Own Ocean Race, originally started from Pwllheli, and now starts at Abersoch. The 1965 race started in unexceptional conditions at 9am on August 4 but during the afternoon, the weather began to deteriorate and by early evening a south-easterly gale had developed.

The Coastguard contacted Capt Jones, the Hon Sec, to report that a number of yachts were missing. *St Albans* was launched at 10.40pm in very bad weather and rough seas and located two of the yachts in the early hours. One was taken in tow, the other escorted back to New Quay.

At first light a helicopter from RAF Brawdy found another yacht in trouble off Aberaeron. *St Albans* was launched again and towed the boat back to New Quay arriving at 10.05am on August 5 – the lifeboat had saved ten lives from the three yachts.

In 1958 Donald Rhoslan Evans was appointed Coxswain with David Winston Evans taking over as Coxswain in September, 1965, aged 26, the youngest ever in Britain to be appointed to the post. Descended from a long line of fishermen, he remained as coxswain until 1994 and was awarded the British Empire Medal in 1985.

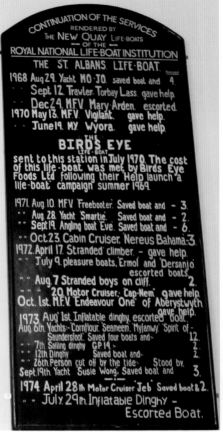

Two more boards recording the services of *St Albans* from 1962 and *Birds Eye* from 1970 until 1974.

Birds Eye

AN ANNOUNCEMENT was made by the RNLI in 1969 that New Quay was to be allocated a new offshore lifeboat. She was a 37ft Oakley class self-righter powered by two 52hp diesel engines giving her a top of speed of 8 knots. Built by Osbornes of Littlehampton at a cost of £38,500, she arrived on station on July 16, 1970. She was named *Birds Eye* after Birds Eye Foods Ltd launched a national appeal during July and August 1969 to Help Launch A Lifeboat. Consumers contributed towards the purchase of a lifeboat by sending in coupons cut from packets of fish fingers.

It was a major promotion for Birds Eye; ten million homes received a colour leaflet regarding the promotion, there were half-page advertisements in the popular national newspapers and a 45-second Captain Birds Eye television commercial. More than 8,500,000 packs carried the tokens. Tesco and Fine Fare ran extensions to the Birds Eye promotion to equip the crew and to buy an inshore rescue boat.

The Oakley lifeboat had come into commission in 1958. Not only was she able to right herself after capsizing, by transferring water ballast to a tank that pulled her back over, she also had much more stability in general than her predecessor. After the success of the Oakley Class boat, all subsequent RNLI All-Weather lifeboats (ALBs) were self-righting.

It had been planned for small sailing vessels to escort the new lifeboat into the harbour but that was not possible because it was low tide. Instead, the ILB with Peter Evans, Trevor Evans, John Evans and Mervyn Thomas on board and the *Ermol*, with Bill Jones in charge, met *Birds Eye* at Llangrannog and escorted her into New Quay. *St Albans* then left for relief duties in Ireland at Cross Haven, County Cork.

The passage of the *Birds Eye* from Poole to New Quay was not without incident; the boat had some fuel problems, and was forced to put in to Exmouth.

The Naming Ceremony and Service of Dedication was held on September 9, 1970, and a good crowd turned out on the pier braving near gale force winds and frequent heavy showers. Both the crowds and the specially invited guests on a platform set up

The Birds Eye Foods Ltd Help Launch a Lifeboat appeal was a major national advertising campaign in 1969 to raise funds for a lifeboat. The image on the right was released after the money was raised and involves some creative licence. Although the boat is named *Birds Eye*, the fleet number 37–10 is incorrect: the real *Birds Eye* is 37–25

A wonderful photograph by Jeff Morris of the early-morning preparations on New Quay pier for the Naming Ceremony and Service of Dedication of the *Birds Eye* on September 7, 1970.

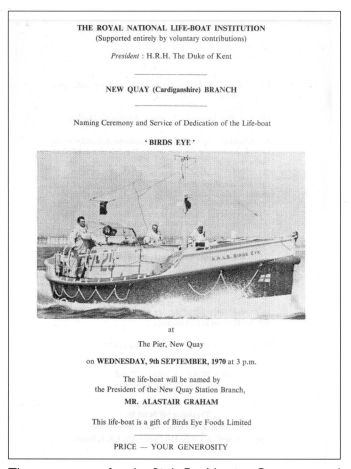

THE ROYAL NATIONAL LIFE-BOAT INSTITUTION
(Supported entirely by voluntary contributions)

President : H.R.H. The Duke of Kent

NEW QUAY (Cardiganshire) BRANCH

Naming Ceremony and Service of Dedication of the Life-boat

'BIRDS EYE'

at

The Pier, New Quay

on **WEDNESDAY, 9th SEPTEMBER, 1970** at 3 p.m.

The life-boat will be named by
the President of the New Quay Station Branch,
MR. ALASTAIR GRAHAM

This life-boat is a gift of Birds Eye Foods Limited

PRICE — YOUR GENEROSITY

The programme for the *Birds Eye* Naming Ceremony and Service of Dedication

on the pier had to take evasive action as heavy seas splashed over the breakwater behind them. The lifeboat was presented to the RNLI by Mr MG Moss, marketing director of Birds Eye Foods Ltd, and accepted on behalf of the lifeboat station by the Hon Sec, Capt J Byron Jones, OBE. The service of dedication was conducted by the Lord Bishop of St David's, the Rt Rev J Richard Richards. Elystan Morgan MP proposed a vote of thanks to all taking part and the boat was then named by the president of the New Quay RNLI, Mr Alastair Graham. The national anthems of Wales and Britain were sung by children of New Quay County Primary School.

Birds Eye's first life-saving service was on August 10, 1971. The Coastguard reported a fishing vessel was in difficulties off Aberporth, and the lifeboat was launched at 1.50pm, reaching the disabled fishing boat, *Freebooter*, with its crew of three, just after 3pm. A towline was secured and she was towed to New Quay where it was low water. Coxswain Evans had to wait until 8.55pm when the lifeboat was able to tow the *Freebooter* into the harbour and then return to the boathouse.

Local knowledge showed its importance on October 23, 1971. The Coastguard reported that flares had been seen four miles north-west of the Lookout. Capt Cosmo Jones, who had taken over as Hon Sec from Capt Byron Jones in 1971, knew that the cabin cruiser *Nereus Bahamas*, which was normally berthed in New Quay harbour, had not returned from a pleasure trip. Capt Jones ordered the *Birds Eye* to be launched at 7pm and after a two-and-a-half hour search, the lifeboat found the three people from

The crew prepare for a trip round the bay after the naming ceremony of the *Birds Eye*. Mechanic Gwilym Davies does some last minute checks at the bow of the boat. Photograph by Jeff Morris.

Alastair Graham

Alastair Graham, who was president of the New Quay branch of the RNLI for many years after the war until the 1970s, has the singular distinction of being the inspiration for two famous characters in 20th-century literature.

He was the closest friend and lover of Evelyn Waugh at Oxford, and is said to be the model for the teddybear-carrying Lord Sebastian Flyte in Brideshead Revisited. A good case has also been made that he was the model for Lord Cut-Glass (a fading, eccentric aristocrat obsessed with time) in Under Milk Wood by Dylan Thomas, who lived in New Quay in 1944 and 1945.

Nephew of the dowager Duchess of Montrose, Graham joined the diplomatic service in 1926 and left in 1933 after a gay sex scandal involving Viscount Tredegar. In 1937, he bought Plas y Wern in Gilfachreda, an impressive, large rambling mansion just outside New Quay where Henry Tudor is reputed to have stayed on his way to the Battle of Bosworth Field in 1485.

Parties there were infamous, with guests including Augustus John, Dylan Thomas, his wife Caitlin and Lord Howard de Walden; Edward VIII was even reported to have made a visit incognito.

Graham played a vital peace-keeping role during a shooting incident in 1945 featured in the film The Edge of Love when William Killick shot at Dylan Thomas. Graham had given Dylan a lift back from the Black Lion in New Quay to Majoda, where he was living, Killick burst into the bungalow spraying shots into the ceiling. Graham calmed down the soldier recently back from war service in Greece by talking about military matters, the war and the state of Greek politics – in Greek.

It is said that Graham played a prominent role after the war in saving the lifeboat station from closure thanks to his aristocratic connections. He sold Plas y Wern in 1958, moving to Rock Street, New Quay, and became a regular at the Dolau Inn. He died in 1982 aged 79 and his ashes were spread at sea.

the *Nereus Bahamas* in an inflatable liferaft. The cabin cruiser had hit a submerged object while travelling at high speed and had sunk within 15 minutes. The three people were landed at New Quay at 11pm

The Coastguard telephoned Capt Jones soon after midnight on August 7, 1972, to report that two boys were stranded on the cliffs between Llangrannog and Penbryn. The Coastguard could not locate the boys; a searchlight from seaward was required and the lifeboat was requested. Once the cliffs were illuminated by the lifeboat the boys were quickly spotted, allowing the Coastguard Cliff Rescue Team to rescue the boys and haul them up the cliffs to safety. The lifeboat was rehoused at 4.30am.

A year later there was high drama during the Regatta. A large number of yachts set out from Pwllheli on August 7, 1973, in the Annual Yacht Race to New Quay. The weather began to deteriorate and shortly after midnight, the Coastguard phoned Capt Jones to express concern for some of the yachts still at sea.

Birds Eye was launched into a southerly gale and heavy seas at 12.45am on August 8 and searched for several hours before finding the yacht *Cornflower*, which had been dismasted and her sails torn to shreds. The crew was rescued and the boat towed to New Quay. The search continued for other yachts as the wind increased to storm force by breakfast time, and four more yachts were found. One was able to continue unaided, but the other three – *Sameen*, *Myfanwy* and *Sarah*, each with a crew of three – were towed to New Quay, one at a time, by the lifeboat, which returned to the boathouse at 1.45pm – 13 hours after being launched.

A majestic Jeff Morris picture of Birds Eye in New Quay Bay after the naming ceremony, with Traethgwyn and Cei Bach in the background. The two men nearest the camera are crewman David Rees (left) and Stan Brett (District Engineer) and on the far side, Picton Williams.

Four-year-old Catherine Mary Evans presents a bouquet to the Duchess of Kent on her visit to the lifeboat station in 1975. Her proud parents, coxswain Winston Evans and his wife Sylwen, look on with members of the crew.

Coxswain Winston Evans introduces the crew to the Duchess of Kent on her visit in 1975. The line-up from the top is: Sydney Fowler, Mervyn Thomas, Michael Davies, David Rees and Dai Davies (universally known as Dai Whiskers). Winston Evans, Sydney Fowler and David Rees were each awarded the RNLI Bronze Medal for an outstanding rescue at Gilfach-yr-Halen in 1966 (see page 46). Mervyn Thomas was awarded the Bronze Medal in 1976 for a rescue at Trwyn Crou (see next page).

Outstanding rescue at Trwyn Crou

THE CREW of the ILB took part in a truly outstanding rescue on July 30, 1974. The drama started at tea-time when the Coastguard informed Capt Jones that a small motorboat had been seen drifting towards the rocks half a mile off Trwyn Crou, an isolated beach four miles south of New Quay.

D-122 was launched at 5.43pm three minutes after the alarm was raised; she was manned by Helmsman Mervyn Thomas and crew members Richard Davies and Richard Phillips. Helmsman Thomas kept as close to shore as possible but in the strong wind and rough seas, progress was slow before they found the motorboat in a very dangerous position close to the rocks at the base of the cliffs.

The ILB approached the boat at 6pm. The man on board said that he and his two companions had dropped anchor after the engine failed, but before it held, the boat had been driven inshore. Two men swam ashore and the lifeboatmen spotted one of them on the rocks, totally exhausted, with heavy surf breaking all around him and in real danger of being swept off the rocks at any moment. The other man seemed to be in no immediate danger, being at the top of the cliffs. Helmsman Thomas took the ILB towards the foot of the cliffs to try to rescue the other man. The Lifeboat Journal takes up the story:

"Helmsman Thomas decided to take the ILB in to the rocks and try to take off the man at the base of the cliff. The sea was rough and confused, with heavy swell running almost at 70° to the direction of the sea, and further aggravated by the reflected waves off the cliff.

The ILB was anchored and backed under power towards the cliffs. On nearing the rocks the engine was stopped, lifted, and the crew continued to back the ILB in under oars. On the first attempt at landing, the boat was lifted by a wave and swept broadside on to a rock, but the crew managed to pull clear by hauling on the anchor cable.

During the second attempt the ILB was completely overwhelmed by a heavy breaking sea and landed full of water on a rocky ledge close to the man in distress. Crew member Richard Phillips got ashore and made his way to the man.

The ILB being perched at an angle on the ledge, some of the water spilled back into the sea and the crew were able to turn her head to sea. Richard Phillips helped the man into the ILB and in doing so damaged the radio aerial; at the same time the boat swept off the ledge, leaving Richard

Phillips on a near-by rock. The next wave washed him off the rock into the sea and he was able to grab a line thrown to him by Helmsman Thomas and was hauled into the boat.

The ILB was pulled clear of the rocks, the engine started and the anchor recovered.

When the ILB went back alongside the small motor boat at anchor, the owner was asked if he wished to be taken off, but he refused to leave his boat. It was now 18.30.

The survivor being in poor shape, suffering from abrasions and exposure, it was decided to land him at Cwmtydu, just over a mile to the north, and Helmsman Thomas told the owner of the boat that he would then return immediately. Because of the damage to the aerial it was not possible to send a radio report to New Quay Coastguard, so, realising that the motor boat was dangerously close to the rocky lee shore, and her owner was determined to remain with her, Helmsman Thomas ordered red flares to be fired to call out the New Quay lifeboat.The survivor was landed at Cwmtydu into the care of D Davies, a Coastguard reporting member. Richard Davies telephoned a situation report through to New Quay Coastguard and requested an ambulance.

The ILB was re-launched, returned to the motor boat and stood by until New Quay lifeboat arrived at 19.05. A tow was passed and the boat was taken to Llangrannog, two miles to the south, where she was safely beached and pulled ashore by tractor. The lifeboat and ILB returned to station and by 21.15 were rehoused and made ready for service.

The man on the cliff was found by a member of the public and placed into the care of the Coastguard. Having swum ashore he managed to scale the cliff and in doing so received severe lacerations to his hands and feet.

This was a remarkable rescue demanding skill, courage and determination from all three lifeboatmen. For his outstanding seamanship, courage and fine leadership, Helmsman Mervyn Thomas was awarded the Bronze Medal by the RNLI, and crewmembers Richard Phillips and Richard Davies were awarded the Institution's Thanks on Vellum.

A NEW D-Class inshore lifeboat *D-238* arrived on station in March 1976 being provided by Hemel Hempstead Round Table, and in its 11 years at New Quay was to be launched 72 times, with 25 lives saved and 61 people in total rescued.

It replaced the first inshore lifeboat at the station, *D-122*, which was launched 56 times with a total of 28 people rescued in its nine years at New Quay. The boat was involved in a number of outstanding rescues.

The new ILB was involved in a fine service on September 9, 1976, shortly after arriving at the station. A yacht *Up Spirits* had anchored overnight in the bay and the next morning, a Force 8 gale was blowing, with rough seas and torrential rain. Capt Jones decided to launch the ILB, on the grounds that she would better fitted for working in the shallow water around the yacht than the *Birds Eye*.

D-238 was launched at 11am with a crew of four to give extra weight. Motor mechanic Mervyn Thomas, the most experienced ILB helmsman at the station, was at the helm and his crewmen were Coxswain Winston Evans, Richard Davies and Morlais Davies. Coxswain Evans recalls it being very rough but he had full confidence in Helmsman Thomas : 'You could go anywhere with Mervyn'. Efforts to beach the yacht failed, and eventually the crew were ready to abandon ship; the yacht was rolling violently and at times, the mast was lying flat on the sea.

The ILB could not get alongside in these conditions, so Helmsman Thomas instructed the two men to jump overboard, one at a time, while he waited with the ILB astern of the yacht.

The men did this and were duly rescued and then landed at New Quay at around 1pm.

For this fine service, the Institution's Thanks on Vellum was awarded to Helmsman Mervyn Thomas, with Vellum Service Certificates being awarded to Winston Evans, Richard Davies and Morlais Davies.

In a separate development, the *Birds Eye* was fitted with radar in 1979.

Heavy snowfalls, the worst for almost 100 years, marked the winter of 1981-82, with many villages being totally cut off for days. Fifteen-foot drifts were reported on the outskirts of New Quay.

Not surprisingly, the lifeboat was particularly busy at this time. The first call-out came at 7.20am on January 11, 1982, after two local doctors who wanted to reach a woman in labour at Llangrannog appealed for help.

Two doctors from New Quay embarked on the *Birds Eye*, but as they neared the village, a signal was received to say that a helicopter had been able to land a doctor to assist the woman, who gave birth to a baby girl and both were flown to Bronglais Hospital, Aberystwyth.

Later it was learned that around 100 children were stranded at the Urdd Camp at Llangrannog, two needing urgent medical supplies, which along with bread and other food, were delivered to the Camp.

As *Birds Eye* headed south, the lifeboatmen noticed a man on top of the cliffs frantically waving his arms. Acting Coxswain Idris

The crew receiving their awards for their part in the rescue of the yacht *Up Spirits* in 1976. From left: Capt Cosmo Jones, Hon Sec; Coxswain Winston Evans; helmsman Mervyn Thomas; crewman Morlais Davies; and Mrs Cosmo Jones.

A celebrity football match was held at New Quay on October 1, 1975, as part of the celebrations to mark the 150th Centenary of the RNLI. The match featured a number of the biggest stars of the time: John Charles, a real legend and all-time best Welsh footballer, turning out with fellow Welsh internationals, his brother Mel, and Ivor Allchurch and Trefor Ford. From the world of rugby, Gareth Edwards, Barry John, David Watkins and Brynmor Williams were on the programme sheet, along with boxer Pat Thomas. A never-to-be repeated event, and for locals, a never-to-be forgotten event. For the record, the Celebrities won 6-5.

Evans took the boat close in shore and it was discovered that the man's family had run out of food for their six-month-old baby. The *Birds Eye* went on to Aberporth to obtain the necessary food and medical supplies, which were safely put ashore at Llangrannog, the lifeboat returning to New Quay at 4.30pm.

Similar missions to deliver food and medical supplies were undertaken to Cymtudu, Llangrannog, Tresaith and Aberporth over the following two days. All these villages have beaches where it was possible take in supplies on a dinghy which the lifeboat had taken on tow.

The Cambrian News reported on January 21, 1982: 'On one occasion a heavy swell was running into Llangrannog and the dinghy carrying three men – David Holeyman, David Williams and Morlais Davies – was overturned in the surf and they were thrown into the sea. After struggling ashore with the medical supplies intact they were looked after by the grateful villagers'.

Morlais Davies recalls it well. 'We went into Llangrannog from the *Birds Eye* on Winston's casting dinghy (there was no inshore life boat on station all-year-round at that time). Nearing the shore, the heavy surf overturned the dinghy and we were thrown six feet deep into the freezing water' [there were lumps of ice floating around in the surf].

Morlais remembers a lady greeting them on the beach with a bottle of whisky, and the men were taken in by the grateful villagers; they were given a bath each and their clothes were dried before they were picked up by the helicopter a few hours later. While all this was going on, Coxswain Winston Evans was already

Crewmen on the quay at New Quay loading the Lifeboat with black bags full of food supplies, mainly bread, and also medical supplies ready to be taken south down the coast to Llangrannog and surrounding villages that had been cut off in the very heavy snowfalls in January 1982. Photograph by crewman Morlais Davies.

Crew members greet the new inshore lifeboat *D-339* at the Handing Over Ceremony and Service of Dedication on September 16, 1987. The Hon Sec Dennis Leworthy is on the right of the photo. The boat saved 24 lives in her first month on station.

at sea in his own boat *Catherine Arden* collecting supplies from Aberystwyth and then delivering them to villages on the way back to New Quay, bringing back essential supplies like yeast for the bakery and among other things, Bass beer for the Dolau Inn. Winston remembers running into a shoal of sprats on the way back. He caught half a ton; the shoal stayed for three weeks, and Winston went back on his boat and caught another half a ton every Sunday for the three weeks.

It was reported that a fishing boat had broken down in bad weather near Llangrannog on July 17, 1985 and the *Birds Eye* with Winston Evans as Coxswain was launched into a Force 6 wind and a four-foot swell at 2.25pm.

The owner was found to be unconscious on the fishing boat and Second Coxswain Idris Evans and lifeboatmen Gregory Boyle and Bernard Evans immediately went on board, where crewman Boyle began mouth-to-mouth resuscitation. An ambulance was called; the man was revived and landed safely at Llangrannog from where he was taken to hospital in Aberystwyth.

The RNLI sent a Letter of Appreciation to the men who had boarded the fishing boat and without whose actions, the unconscious man would almost certainly have died.

In the 1986 New Year's Honours, Winston Evans, Coxswain of the New Quay lifeboat since 1965, was awarded the British Empire Medal. Ever-modest he said, 'It helps to be a fisherman when you are doing rescue work – you get to know the area very well.'

In July 1987, a new inshore lifeboat was sent to New Quay. *D-339* was paid for from the proceeds of a concert in March, 1987, in aid of the RNLI at St David's Hall, Cardiff, featuring the Morriston Orpheus Choir.

The new ILB was launched on service for the first time on August 7 to rescue a capsized sailing dinghy and six days later was called out again to aid a rowing boat in difficulties north east of New Quay with two teenagers on board. The ILB towed the rowing boat into Aberaeron Harbour and then returned to station at 10.00pm. *D-339* was very busy from the start and was involved in eight rescues in her first month on station.

In a Handing Over Ceremony and Service of Dedication at the boathouse on September 16, Mr Raymond Cory, deputy chairman of the Institution, handed the boat into the care of the New Quay Station. It was accepted by the Hon Sec Dennis Leworthy and a service of dedication was conducted by the Rector of New Quay, the Rev David Lloyd.

On January 28, 1990, *Birds Eye* was withdrawn from service. She was launched for the last time exactly a week before that on January 21. A sailboarder was reported in difficulties off Aberporth in rough seas; the sailboarder was rescued by helicopter which had been called, and *Birds Eye* returned to the Station for the last time at 5pm.

Her replacement was another 37ft Oakley Class lifeboat, the *Calouste Gulbenkian*, previously stationed at Weston-super-Mare. She served at New Quay for 12 months launching six times, although not being credited with any effective services.

Birds Eye on the turntable on New Quay town beach. On the right of the picture, one of the two balancing poles which were used to support the boat and keep her upright while being hauled on to the turntable to allow the boat to be pulled back onto the carriage. The tractor then pushed *Birds Eye* back to the station. This was a job for strong men.

Coxswain Winston Evans is presented with his British Empire Medal by the Lord Lieutenant of Dyfed, Sir David Courtenay Mansel Lewis, in the Memorial Hall in 1986.
Winston's family joins the line-up: Sylwen and their two children Catherine Mary and Jonathan. Crew members look on from the stage.

Detail of the *Birds Eye*, which is now on display at the RNLI's Seawatch Centre at Moelfre, Anglesey.

She herself was replaced by the ex-Hastings lifeboat *Fairlight*, another 37ft Oakley. In 1991, the RNLI announced that New Quay was to be allocated one of the new high-speed Mersey Class all-weather lifeboats, which necessitated the building of a new boathouse and *Fairlight* had to be kept out on the beach while the new lifeboat station was built. *Fairlight* was at New Quay for 15 months, her first service being on July 11, 1991, when flares were sighted three miles north east of Aberporth. In rough seas, the lifeboat located a yacht *Kamille* with three people on board, who were unsure of their position. They were escorted back to New Quay.

The former Hastings lifeboat, *Fairlight*, was on station at New Quay from January 1991 to April 1992. Pictured here near Target Rock, she was kept out on the beach while the new lifeboat house was built.

Roger Bryan

The Mersey

The 12-metre Mersey Class All Weather Lifeboat was designed and developed by the RNLI for stations where variable tides demand that the lifeboat be launched from a carriage. New Quay is one of 22 such stations. New Quay's Mersey Class boat 12-15 *Frank and Lena Clifford of Stourbridge* came on station in 1992, and is pictured here 20 years later in 2012 looking as new as if she had come straight

out of the paint shop. The lifeboat is housed on a carriage in the boathouse; launching is a quick operation in which lifeboat and carriage are pushed by the Talus tractor from the boathouse into a suitable depth of water where the boat is partially floated and moved clear from the carriage.

The Mersey is powered by two 285 hp Caterpillar 3208T turbo-charged V8 four-stroke diesel engines giving a maximum speed of 17.5 knots, twice the speed of the Oakley and Rother Class lifeboats she replaced and

half the weight of the Tyne Class lifeboat, allowing her to be towed by tractor over soft sand. The propellers are protected by partial tunnels and substantial bilge keels that make her ideal for use in shallow waters. Should the lifeboat be capsized the inherent bouyancy of the watertight wheelhouse means she can self-right in six seconds. Fuel capacity is 1,100 litres (around 245 gallons) with a range of 150 nautical miles. She has a crew of six and can carry an X Boat inflatable which she can deploy at sea.

Frank and Lena Clifford of Stourbridge

IN 1991, the RNLI announced that New Quay was to receive one of the new high-speed 12-metre Mersey Class all-weather lifeboats, which necessitated the building of a new boathouse for the new boat, the ILB and the launching tractor. There was a delay in putting the boat on station: the boathouse which had been thought only to need modification to house the new boat, actually had to be demolished and totally re-built.

When work on the re-built boathouse was finished, the new lifeboat was placed on service on April 8, 1992. She cost £455,000 to build and fit out, and was to be called *Frank and Lena Clifford of Stourbridge,* being provided out of a legacy of the late Mr Frank Clifford, of Stourbridge, Worcestershire, along with other bequests and gifts.

Frank Clifford was the owner and managing director of an industrial company near Stourbridge in the West Midlands. He and his wife Lena (née Wood), a violin and viola player who played with the City of Birmingham Symphony Orchestra for many years and taught at the Birmingham School of Music from 1946 until 1970, were good friends with Mrs Pam Grice, the social secretary of the Stourbridge branch of the RNLI.

It was with Mrs Grice and her husband Aubrey that Mr Clifford attended the annual RNLI dinner at Stourbridge in 1983 where the speaker was one Harry Jones, the 65-year-old former coxswain of the Hoylake lifeboat on the Wirral. And what a speaker, by the sound of it.

A widower, Mr Clifford was 86 at the time and had decided to leave his estate to the Wildfowl & Wetlands Trust at Slimbridge. That was until he heard Mr Jones's talk on the work of the RNLI: he was so impressed that he changed his will, leaving two-thirds of his estate of £441,127 (gross) to the RNLI and one-third to the WWT. He died in 1985 aged 88 and Mrs Grice was quoted in the local paper: 'I couldn't believe it when the solicitor told me after the funeral that he had left all that money to the RNLI'.

As soon as the local RNLI committee learned of the legacy, they took a keen interest in how it was used. Sue Coombes, Hon Secretary of the Stourbridge branch, has unearthed the following information from the minutes of the branch.

Over she goes! The boat was launched for the first time at Cowes on March 27, 1991, and underwent a successful self-righting trial that day.

Frank and Lena Clifford of Stourbridge under construction. The hull was made of FRC (Fibre Reinforced Composite) moulded at Green Marine, of Lymington, and then fitted out here in the photo at FBM Marine Ltd, Cowes. While the lifeboat waited to go on station in 1991, she was used for training purposes on the south coast, and on one occasion assisted the Alderney lifeboat in the Channel Islands in the rescue of the crew of a sinking trawler. New Quay RNLI Mechanic Mervyn Thomas said afterwards: 'It's a lovely boat and handles extremely well. It will enable us to answer any emergency in half the time'.

Crewman Michael Jones and Mechanic Mervyn Thomas on *Frank and Lena Clifford of Stourbridge* at the Boat Show at Earls Court, London, in January, 1992. She was mounted on her special launching carriage, and exhibited along with the Talus MB-H, a new launching tractor T113 purpose-built for the New Quay station.

'It was hoped from the outset that the monies would go toward a lifeboat named after Frank Clifford and his wife Lena. At a meeting in 1987, Stourbridge branch secretary Chris Fonteyn asked whether 'of Stourbridge' could be affixed to the name and the suggestion was passed on to the regional organiser.

'At the same meeting, it was recorded that the RNLI would receive one quarter of the estate of Miss Mary Heathcock, a teacher at St Joseph's Primary School in Stourbridge, a long-standing RNLI supporter. The legacy amounted to £12,184 and it was agreed that this should also go towards the new lifeboat.

'In 1989, the RNLI suggested that the legacy should be put towards a Tyne class lifeboat stationed at Wicklow in Ireland. However, the executors of the Clifford legacy at Stourbridge expressed the view that the money should fund a Mersey Class lifeboat, somewhere in Britain where it would be more easily accessible to visitors from the Midlands. The RNLI agreed with this, and eventually the Mersey boat was allocated to New Quay'.

Mrs Coombes said: 'The Stourbridge RNLI branch is very proud of having Stourbridge as part of the name of the New Quay lifeboat. It not only reflects the strong support for the lifeboat service from the landlocked town over many years, but the lifeboat that bears its name also serves both as a focal point and an incentive to the branch's fundraising efforts, with local people being encouraged to visit New Quay to see the boat for themselves'.

At the Naming Ceremony and Service of Dedication on June 25, 1992, Anna Hartley, daughter of Second Coxswain Steve Hartley, presented a bouquet to Mrs Grice before the boat was presented to the RNLI by Mr Aubrey Grice on behalf of the executors of Mr Clifford's estate. The boat was accepted by Mr Raymond Cory, deputy chairman of the RNLI, who handed the boat over to the Hon Sec of New Quay Lifeboat Station, Mr Dennis Leworthy. The Bishop of St David's, the Rt Rev J Ivor Rees, conducted the service of dedication after which Mrs Grice named the boat *Frank and Lena Clifford of Stourbridge*, the boat being launched to great cheers from the large crowd.

Frank and Lena Clifford of Stourbridge is numbered 12–15: 12 denotes a Mersey Class lifeboat, and 15 is the number of the boat in the RNLI's fleet of Mersey Class boats.

The new lifeboat had been in action five days before the naming ceremony. Having been called out to assist a yacht in rough seas, she was returning to New Quay when the Coastguard asked her to assist the crew of the yacht *Magwr*, which was dragging her anchor off New Quay harbour. The lifeboat men got a line aboard the yacht and towed her into the harbour.

Later that summer, the inshore lifeboat was very busy on August 12, 1992. At 3.15pm, *D-339* went to the aid of a windsurfer in difficulties in choppy seas and a strong wind in the bay. The surfer having been rescued, an inflatable airbed was then reported to have capsized, two people being thrown in the water.

The ILB put to sea immediately and rescued the pair, landing them on the beach at 3.45pm. Twenty-five minutes later, the ILB was relaunched again after another airbed was seen to have capsized: the two people were rescued and landed back on the beach at 4.30pm.

Five Men in a Boat: The crew that brought *Frank and Lena Clifford of Stourbridge* back on passage from Cowes to New Quay in 1992. From left: Dan Potter (soon to be coxswain), Winston Evans (Coxswain), Michael Jones, Roger Davies (later to become Hon Sec) and Mervyn Thomas (Mechanic).

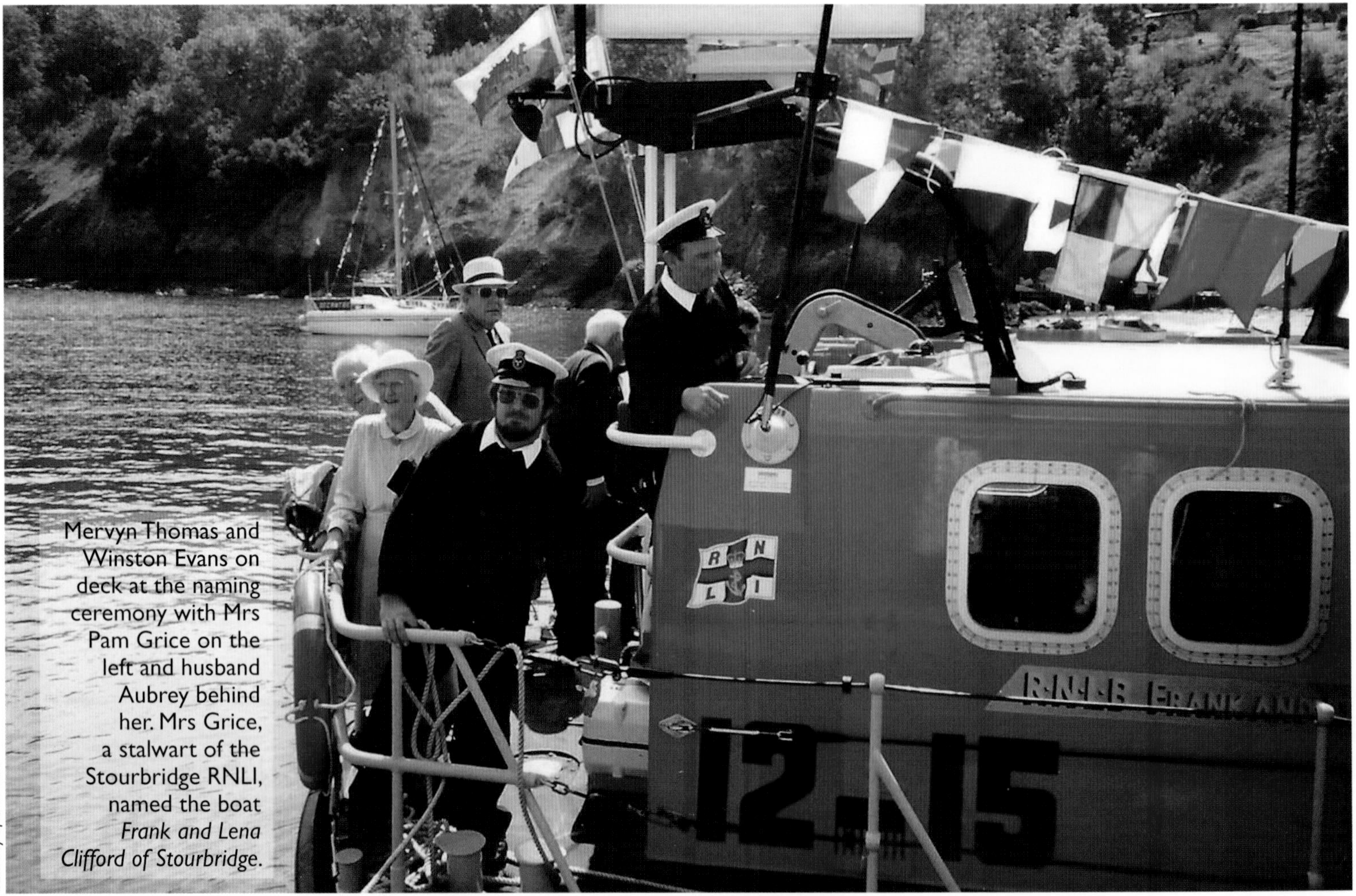

Mervyn Thomas and Winston Evans on deck at the naming ceremony with Mrs Pam Grice on the left and husband Aubrey behind her. Mrs Grice, a stalwart of the Stourbridge RNLI, named the boat *Frank and Lena Clifford of Stourbridge*.

Courtesy of the RNLI

Frank and Lena Clifford of Stourbridge on the slipway at the Naming Ceremony and Service of Dedication. The boat was launched to great cheers and the BBC was on hand to preserve the occasion for posterity.

Royal National **Lifeboat** Institution

New Quay Lifeboat Station
Gorsaf Bad Achub Cei Newydd
Seremoni Enwi a Gwasanaeth Cyflwyno
"Frank and Lena Clifford of Stourbridge"
Dydd Iau 25ain Mehefin 1992

Pris y Rhaglen – EICH HAELIONI CHI
Price of Programme – YOUR GENEROSITY

NEW QUAY LIFEBOAT CREW AND SHORE HELPERS

Coxswain : WINSTON EVANS, BEM
Second Coxswain : DANIEL POTTER
Mechanic : MERVYN THOMAS
Head Launcher : IAN HIDES
Tractor Driver : VINCENT THOMAS
Second Tractor Driver : JOHN EVANS

CREW MEMBERS

SCOTT BOWEN	MARCUS HEADLEY
GREGORY BOYLE	CHRISTIAN JONES
JAMES BRIDDON	MICHAEL JONES
FREDDIE DAVIES	REES TOM JONES
ROGER DAVIES	GARETH POTTER
JONATHAN EVANS	STEPHEN SWAN
TONY EVANS	CARL THOULD
TREVOR EVANS	ADRIAN TURNER
STEVE HARTLEY	PAUL YATES

SHORE HELPERS

JOHN BRIDDON	JOHN LEWORTHY
ALUN EVANS	ROGER PERKS
HOWARD EVANS	MATHEW THOMAS
JOHN HICKS	STEPHEN THOULD
ROBERT LEWIS	

STATION BRANCH OFFICIALS

President : Captain B. JONES, OBE
Chairman : Captain D. BOWEN
Honorary Secretary : Mr. D. LEWORTHY
Honorary Treasurer : Mr. A. GRIFFITHS

LADIES GUILD OFFICIALS

President : Mrs. E. EVANS
Chairman : Mrs. R. TIMAEUS, JP
Honorary Treasurer : Mrs. J. THOMAS
Honorary Secretary : Mrs. P. BRYANT
Souvenir Secretary : Miss J. JONES

Frank and Lena Clifford of Stourbridge was soon called into action; it is worthy of note that the photograph was taken from the pier, before the lifeboat had properly left the harbour. Photograph by Emyr Rhys Williams.

AFTER reports that a car had gone over the cliffs at Llangrannog on July 4, 1993, *Frank and Lena Clifford of Stourbridge* was launched at 9.15am. Two people had swum out from Llangrannog to help but had themselves got into difficulties.

Two of the lifeboat crew jumped into the choppy sea, and brought one person back to the lifeboat suffering from shock.

The second person was found on nearby rocks, and he too was taken onto the lifeboat. A dinghy came out from Llangrannog and took the rescued people back to the shore, a helicopter then flying them to hospital. The lifeboat returned to station at 12.30pm.

In June 1994, the station at New Quay became an all-year-round ILB station and in 1995, received a new inshore lifeboat. This was paid for by the London firm of lawyers, Sinclair, Roche & Temperley, out of money raised during a concert at St Paul's Cathedral to mark the 60th anniversary of the company and also the centenary of The City of London branch of the RNLI.

At the Naming Ceremony and Service of Dedication at New Quay on September 2, 1995, the boat, *D-476* was handed over to the RNLI by Mr Nigel Beavan, of St Paul's Cathedral, and after a service of dedication conducted by the Rev Roy Davies, rector of New Quay, the lifeboat was named *Corydd* by Mrs Jackie Beavan.

In Welsh, *Corydd* means chorister, and seems an absolutely appropriate name for a boat with such a connection to St Paul's Cathedral.

Corydd was launched on May 7, four days after being placed on service, after a 21ft RIB *Lion Heart* with four people on board

had broken down three miles off New Quay. The disabled boat was towed back to the harbour.

Frank and Lena Clifford of Stourbridge was launched in April 1995 to go to the aid of the yacht *Still Water*, which had mechanical problems 25 miles north-west of New Quay. The lifeboat reached the yacht at 4.10pm, and in calm seas, towed the boat and the two people on board back to New Quay where she was berthed at 8.16pm.

There were two late-night, early-morning calls in the summer of 1995. On the evening of June 24, the cabin cruiser *Fox* with five people on board broke down off Llangrannog. *Frank and Lena Clifford of Stourbridge* was launched at 9.18pm and subsequently towed the disabled boat back to New Quay, returning to the boathouse at midnight. Cabin cruiser *Ystwyth*, a former Aberystwyth lifeboat, with two people on board broke down at Llangrannog in the early hours of July 24. The ALB was launched again at 5.14am and towed the disabled boat into New Quay harbour at 8.40am.

The crew of Cardigan's C-class inshore lifeboat took part in an excellent service on August 26, 1996. Three people and a dog had become cut off by the tide at Penbryn. Lifeguard Simon Jury who was on his surfboard at the time alerted the Coastguard. A near gale force wind had developed, whipping up the seas, and the highest tide of the year was due in two and a half hours' time. Cardigan's ILB was launched at 6.55pm and *Frank and Lena Clifford of Stourbridge* was launched 40 minutes later.

With great skill and courage, the Cardigan lifeboatmen assisted by Simon Jury, succeeded in rescuing the three stranded people

Daniel Potter has been Coxswain at New Quay since 1994 when he took over from Winston Evans. He comes from a long line of family members connected with the lifeboat; his great-uncle, Frederick Shaylor, was Coxswain from 1918 to 1935.

all of whom were wet, cold and very frightened. With some difficulty, the rescued people were transferred to the *Frank and Lena Clifford of Stourbridge* from the Cardigan ILB. During the nine-mile passage back to New Quay all three rescued people suffered from severe sea-sickness in the extremely rough seas.

The RNLI's Chief of Operations later sent a Letter of Appreciation to New Quay Coxswain Daniel Potter and his crew 'for the assistance you gave to the Cardigan ILB which was operating in conditions close on the limits for this class of lifeboat'.

A catamaran capsized off Tresaith, eight miles south-west of New Quay, early on the evening of September 5, 1997, after being dismasted in very choppy seas and strong winds. ILB *Corydd* was launched at 6.15pm, rescuing the three people and handing them over to paramedics on the beach

In the afternoon of July 27, 1999, *Corydd* was launched in a choppy sea and a strong, gusty easterly wind after a sailing dinghy with three men and three children on board capsized half a mile north of New Quay Head. The six were quickly rescued and the dinghy righted and towed back to the harbour.

In very heavy seas and a near gale force north westerly wind, it took one and a half hours for *Frank and Lena Clifford of Stourbridge* to reach a yacht in difficulties 20 miles from New Quay on December 16, 2000. Two lifeboatmen, Rees-Tom Jones and Marc Rees, managed to board the yacht *Snowscamp*, despite both boats rolling and pitching violently in the heavy seas. The crew of two were suffering from exhaustion and were very sea-sick but the lifeboatmen secured a towline and set off for Fishguard. At 6.30pm, the tow was handed over to the Fishguard lifeboat and *Frank and Lena Clifford of Stourbridge* arrived back at New Quay at 9.42pm after an exhausting five-hour service. At least there was a good meal waiting for the crew – it was the night of the Christmas Dinner.

The Coastguard reported on July 27, 2001, that a party of schoolchildren and teachers were cut off by the tide near Llanrhystud. The ILB *Corydd* was launched at 5.25pm, followed ten minutes later by the *Frank and Lena Clifford of Stourbridge*. *Corydd* found 12 teenagers and two teachers stranded in a cove, and made a number of trips to ferry them out to the ALB which was waiting off-shore. The two lifeboats then headed for Llanrhystud beach where the *Corydd* took everyone ashore.

The lifeboat was launched at 8.46pm on July 19, 2003, after concerns that the *Teymar* from New Quay had not been seen or heard of for almost 12 hours. Milford Haven Coastguard asked the lifeboat to search northwards up to and beyond Aberystwyth. At 6.35am the next morning, Barmouth lifeboat located the *Teymar* north of Abersytwyth six miles off shore suffering from engine failure. The tow was transferred to the *Frank and Lena Clifford of Stourbridge*, the lifeboat returning with the casualty at 9.35am.

The All Weather Lifeboat was called into action on August 5 at 11.50pm to assist the ILB D-476 *Corydd* in saving six people trapped on a cliff two miles north east of the station. The ALB stood by and lit the scene while the casualties were lowered in to the ILB by the Coastguard Cliff Rescue Team. All six were safely transferred to the lifeboat which returned to station at 2.30am.

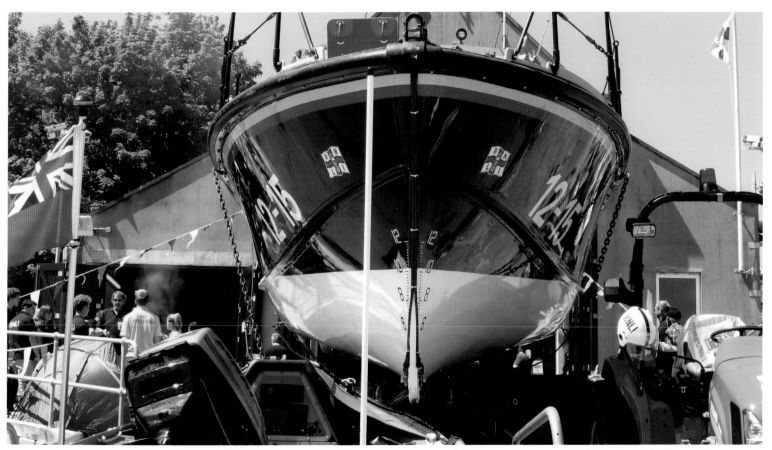

Mersey Class lifeboat 12–15 *Frank and Lena Clifford of Stourbridge* was the sparkling centre of attention at this Open Day at the boathouse. When the station was redecorated in 2010, Roger Couch, LOM, insisted that the signature red and yellow RNLI stripes painted on the upper part of the hull of the lifeboat below the gunwhales should be replicated around the boathouse walls, one metre off the ground. It was an idea that has been widely copied in other boathouses since.

Courtesy of the RNLI

The Duke of Kent, President of the RNLI, visited the New Quay station in 1995 and was introduced to Daniel Potter, Coxswain, and Mervyn Thomas, Station Mechanic. The Duke was accompanied by George Rawlinson (right), who is now the RNLI's Operations Director.

CORYDD

Catherine Evans

Inshore LIfeboat *D-476, Corydd,* at her Naming Ceremony and Service of Dedication in 1995. Corydd means chorister in Welsh, the money for the boat having been raised at a concert at St Paul's Cathedral, London. The original nameplate is inset into the picture. *Corydd* was launched 85 times, saving 36 lives, and rescuing 127 people.

THERE were 23 people on board the locally-owned coastal cruise trip boat *Ermol 6* on July 3, 2005, when she fouled her propellers near Birds' Rock and was drifting toward the cliffs. The lifeboat was paged at 2.01pm, *Frank and Lena Clifford of Stourbridge* was launched eight minutes later, and proceeding at full-speed, reached the scene at 2.21pm. *Ermol 6* was then towed back to New Quay and brought alongside in the harbour where the relieved passengers were safely disembarked.

The ILB *D-616 Amy Lea* came on station in 2004 and a service on August 14, 2005, surely set some sort of record. The crew was paged by Milford Haven Coastguard at 7.22am after a person was reported in the water just outside the harbour having being washed overboard from a small dinghy while trying to board a yacht. The *Amy Lea* reached the casualty at 7.23am – one minute after the call came though. The casualty was taken to the beach and then by ambulance to hospital. The ILB returned to station at 7.35am.

Frank and Lena Clifford of Stourbridge was launched in thick fog at 11.37am on April 15, 2007. The 22-foot Stewart Stevens motor cruiser *CJ* had suffered engine failure and alerted the coastguard, but was unable to give her precise position due to the fog. The ALB used radio Direction Finding equipment and radar to locate the craft half a mile off Aberporth Reef where she had anchored safely. Arriving on the scene at 12.32pm, the lifeboat took the boat under tow and placed it on a mooring in New Quay Harbour at 2.05pm. Two people on board were transferred to the lifeboat and landed on the main beach at New Quay as the lifeboat was being recovered.

Both lifeboats were called out at 6.27pm on August 21 following a report of people in the sea at Llangrannog. Arriving on the scene, the ILB – *Amy Lea* – rescued a woman from the sea who was feared to be suffering from hypothermia and shock. She was in need of medical attention and quickly transferred to *Frank and Lena Clifford of Stourbridge* . A Sea King helicopter from RAF Valley – Rescue 122 – was tasked to remove the casualty and on arrival at the scene, put its paramedic winchman on board the ALB. Following assessment, the casualty was then transferred up to the helicopter and taken to Bronglais Hospital, Aberystwyth.

Five days later, *Frank and Lena Clifford of Stourbridge* was launched at 10.08am after a call to the Milford Haven Coastguard to assist a vessel, *Sea Warrior*, with seven people on board that had lost engine power two miles off Aberarth. The lifeboat attached a tow to the vessel arriving back in New Quay at 11.27am.

Amy Lea was called out on a canine rescue mission on December 11 at 12.20pm following reports to Milford Haven Coastguard by the owner of a dog that had fallen over the cliff south of Llangrannog. (The dog had fallen, not the owner). On arrival at the scene, the ILB located the dog and guided the Coastguard Cliff Rescue team to the precise position. The dog, called Rocket, was not injured and lifted to the top of the cliff to be returned to a very grateful owner.

Frank and Lena Clifford of Stourbridge leads relief lifeboat *Margaret Jean* into New Quay harbour on July 23, 1993. The Mersey-class relief boat under the command of second coxswain Daniel Potter had come from Holyhead, where *Frank and Lena Clifford of Stourbridge* was to go for a refit. The relief boat was on station for two weeks. Photograph by Nicholas Leach.

Sea King Rescue Helicopter 169 from Chivenor on exercise out in New Quay Bay with *Frank and Lena Clifford of Stourbridge*. The lifeboat station is in the background. Photograph by Brett Stones.

A magnificent photo, taken during an exercise in 2010, of a Search and Rescue Sea King helicopter from 22 Squadron, the Royal Marine Base, Chivenor, Devon, with the terraces of New Quay in the background.

The photo was taken by Ben Billingham, Station Mechanic, aboard *Frank and Lena Clifford of Stourbridge*.

Crewman Simon Williams and Mechanic Ben Billingham aboard Sea King Search and Rescue Helicopter 169 after being winched up from *Frank and Lena Clifford of Stourbridge*.

A winchman from Sea King Search and Rescue 169 takes a nonchalant trip across New Quay Bay as the helicopter approaches the lifeboat on the annual joint exercise. The photograph was taken from the *Frank and Lena Clifford of Stourbridge*

Audrey Lawson Johnston and the Lusitania

Audrey Warren Pearl was just three months old when she survived the sinking of the Cunard liner *Lusitania* torpedoed by a German U-boat off the coast of Ireland on May 7, 1915. Eighty-nine years later to the day, on May 7, 2004, the Hon Mrs Audrey Lawson Johnston was guest of honour at the Naming Ceremony and Service of Dedication for a new inshore lifeboat at New Quay, *D-616 Amy Lea* named after her American mother Amy Lea Pearl. Both Audrey and Amy Lea were survivors of the *Lusitania* – one of the largest maritime disasters of the First World War.

Audrey was born in New York City in 1915, the fourth child of Warren and Amy Pearl. Shortly after her birth, her father, a surgeon major in the American Army, was instructed to report to the US Embassy in London. She was three months old when she was carried aboard the RMS *Lusitania* in New York in May with her parents, three siblings and two nursemaids.

Six days into the journey and only hours from arriving at Liverpool, *Lusitania* was hit by a German torpedo at 2.15pm on Friday, May 7. In the crush and panic, the parents lost contact with their children. Nursemaid Alice Lines, an 18-year-old English girl, was feeding Audrey when the torpedo hit. She tied the baby in a shawl round her neck and took Audrey's five-year-old brother Stuart by the hand saying, 'Come along, we won't wait for anything . . . Hang on to me whatever happens'. Stuart screamed: 'I don't want to be drowned. I don't want to be drowned'.

THE RMS *Lusitania* was launched by the Cunard Line in 1907 at a time of fierce competition on the North Atlantic ocean liner route. A beautiful ship with four funnels and six decks of passenger accommodation above the waterline, she was as luxurious as any liner afloat and was at one time, the world's biggest ship.

When she left Pier 54 in New York City for Liverpool on what was to be her final voyage, the war in the Atlantic was intensifying. Germany had declared the seas around the UK a war zone, and on the afternoon of May 7, 1915, *Lusitania* was torpedoed by German submarine *U-20* 11 miles off Kinsale Head on the southern coast of Ireland.

A total of 1198 people lost their lives. Eighteen minutes after the torpedo hit the starboard bow of the ship, the bow struck the seabed and as in the sinking of the *Titanic*, the stern rose in the air before sliding beneath the waves. There were 764 survivors. This attack on a non-military ship without warning (although the Germans may have had reasons to treat the *Lusitania* as a naval vessel – it was later discovered she was carrying war munitions) caused a storm of protest in America, and was a big influence in the US declaring war two years later.

Crew members with the inshore lifeboat *D-616 Amy Lea* before her last exercise in 2012. Pictured (from left) are: Charlie Turner, Elis Jones, Bernie Davies, Peter Yates, Dylan Price, Tim Harrison, Ben Billingham, Simon Rigby and Jolyon Quayle. The lifeboat was launched 114 times rescuing 91 people in its eight years on station.

Alice recalled that she struggled and 'had a hill to climb to get to the lifeboat'. She said a sailor forcibly put Stuart in the lifeboat, which then began to be lowered. Alice, hysterical by this stage, pushed her way through and in desperation, jumped for the lifeboat but missed, landing in the water with Audrey still tied to her. Alice and Audrey were saved by Alice's long hair by which she was dragged into the lifeboat.

'The suction of the liner was pulling us back. Every time the oars went forward, we were going as if we were going to be drawn under. Eventually, we got away and I saw the funnels one by one disappearing. I saw all those lifeboats – the lifeboat I was in was the only one saved on that side . . . The sea was as calm as a pond. I don't think anybody would be alive now if it hadn't been a lovely calm day'.

Chillingly she said, 'There was a submarine on the surface watching us. I saw those sailors watching all those bodies of people and wreckage . . .'

They were rescued some time later by an Irish government patrol boat. The rest of the family was split up. Audrey's father Warren Pearl spent three hours in the water and was eventually landed at Queenstown about eight hours after the sinking, to be reunited with his wife Amy who had been rescued separately by a tramp steamer. Together they resumed the search for their missing children. They tracked down Alice with Audrey and Stuart, but their sisters Amy and Susan as well as nanny Greta Lorenson were lost.

After arriving in Britain, the family settled in London. Audrey was presented at Court in 1933 on her 18th birthday, meeting Queen

The Hon Mrs Audrey Lawson Johnston naming the new ILB *Amy Lea* after her mother; both were survivors of the sinking of the *Lusitania* in 1915. The ceremony took place on the 89th anniversary of the disaster. Her daughter Primrose Hudson is at her side.

The ILB crew put the *Audrey LJ* through her paces for the first time in 2012. From left: Simon Rigby, Ben Billingham and helmsman Peter Yates.

Mary; her 21st birthday present was a trip on the maiden voyage of Cunard's new liner *Queen Mary* to visit family in New York.

In 1946 she married Hugh Lawson Johnston who came from an illustrious family – his grandfather had invented the meat extract Bovril.

Mrs Audrey Lawson Johnston remained close to Alice Lines until Alice's death in 1997 at the age of 100. Like her mother, Audrey was an active charity fundraiser throughout her life, especially for the RNLI and raised £26, 000 for the new lifeboat at New Quay.

In a BBC interview towards the end of her life, she said: 'I was put on this earth for some reason. I was saved for some reason – I hope I'm living up to worth being saved'.

In 2012, *Amy Lea* was replaced by a new ILB, *D-754 Audrey LJ*, named by her family after Mrs Audrey Lawson Johnston, who having been the youngest survivor from the *Lusitania*, was the oldest living surviver when she died in January, 2011, aged 95.

Roger Couch, Lifeboat Operations Manager at New Quay, said: 'Mrs Lawson Johnston was a dedicated supporter and fundraiser for the RNLI throughout her life and developed a particular interest in the New Quay station.

'It was a real pleasure to meet with her during the naming of *Amy Lea* and we were humbled to hear that her family was keen to help fund another lifeboat for our station. It was a proud moment for all the volunteer crew at the station to witness the new lifeboat being named *Audrey LJ* in honour of one of our most dedicated supporters'.

At the ceremony on October 27, the lifeboat was officially named by Amy Crocker, Mrs Lawson Johnston's eldest grand-daughter.

The new lifeboat designed and developed by the RNLI makes good use of space for a crew of three. A GPS plotter assists in the navigation of the boat, which is powered by a 50hp engine giving a top speed of 25 knots.

Mr Couch said: 'This is a safe, speedy and manoeuvreable craft which will enable us to respond well to inshore incidents.'

WHEN the *Lusitania* was sunk, the local lifeboat, the Courtmacsherry pulling and sailing boat *Kezia Gwilt*, was launched. There was no wind, and it took the boat three and a half hours to row the 14 miles to the scene of the wreck. They could only pick up dead bodies.

A copy of the Return of Service for the Courtmacsherry lifeboat recording her launch to the sinking of the *Lusitania* was presented to New Quay Lifeboat Station by Courtmacsherry Station at the *Amy Lea* service of dedication on May 7, 2004.

It is proudly displayed in the crewroom along with another link with the *Lusitania* and the Courtmacsherry station – a framed print of the Cunard liner signed by the American artist, Ken Marschall, and also by Audrey Lawson Johnston and Alice Lines, which is due to go to Courtmacsherry for an exhibition in 2015 to commemorate the 100th anniversary of the sinking of the *Lusitania*.

Inshore lifeboat *D-754 Audrey LJ* being put through her paces soon after coming on station in September 2012. The crew of four from left: Peter Yates, Sarah Perry, Elis Jones and Brett Stones are getting a real soaking by the look of it. Photograph by Morlais Davies.

A dramatic shot of the *Frank and Lena Clifford of Stourbridge* taken by a holidaymaker on Town Beach at the start of a shout to go to the aid of a catamaran stranded on Cardigan Bar. It was a choppy sea, only a few yards out from the harbour.

Previous page: A memorable image by Emyr Rhys Williams of the All Weather Lifeboat 12-15 on bad weather exercise. The photograph was used in 2011 on the cover of a book, Mayday Mayday, that tied in with a TV series of the same name.

This is a unique photograph of all the maritime emergency services in New Quay. It was taken at the launch of the Ceredigion Lifeguards service in 2008. In the picture (from left) are: HM New Quay Coastguards, county councillors, the Ceredigion Lifeguards, New Quay lifeboat officials and local councillors, the Inshore Lifeboat and crew, the Talus tractor and drivers, and on the lifeboat the crew of the *Frank and Lena Clifford of Stourbridge*.

THE NEW QUAY Lifeboat was involved in a dangerous, courageous and exhausting service in severe gale force winds more than 20 miles out to sea on September 6, 2008.

Milford Haven Coastguard had received a call from *Galasma*, a 30-foot Southerly on passage to Aberystwyth with five people on board. The yacht had lost all engine power and was encountering difficulties in the heavy seas and extremely bad weather.

Frank and Lena Clifford of Stourbridge was launched at 12.02pm in gale conditions, a very rough sea and poor visibility, to assist *Galasma*, which was reported to be 16 miles west of Aberystwyth.

In fact, when *Frank and Lena Clifford of Stourbridge* reached *Galasma*, the yacht was around 23 miles out to sea. The lifeboat attached a towline and headed for Aberystwyth. The Force 9 severe gale dictated a very slow towing speed and with a falling tide, it was decided that entry into Aberystwyth harbour was impossible.

An alternative port was needed and after consultations with coastguards at Milford and Holyhead, it was agreed that the New Quay lifeboat should alter course north towards Pwllheli and that the Pwllheli lifeboat would launch to take over the tow at an agreed rendezvous point.

The New Quay towline was successfully transferred to Pwllheli's Mersey Class Lifeboat *Lilly & Vincent Anthony* at 3.50pm and both lifeboats started on their passages back to their respective stations. The New Quay ALB returned home at 5.30pm, having been at sea for five and half hours. After assisting the yacht to moor safely in Pwllheli Marina, the Pwllheli ALB returned to station at 9.30pm having been at sea for seven hours.

The photo of the *Galasma* and the Pwllheli lifeboat opposite was taken from *Frank and Lena Clifford of Stourbridge* by New Quay crew member Hanna Nuuttila, a marine biologist carrying out research into the dolphins and porpoises in Cardigan Bay. It won the RNLI Photograph of the Year competition in 2008 and she was presented with her award at the London International Boat Show in 2009. The photograph was titled Seconds From Disaster and brilliantly captures the extremely rough state of the sea during the rescue.

She said: 'I'm totally surprised to win the title of RNLI photographer of the year because my fellow crew mates in New Quay entered the image on my behalf. It's an honour to be recognised, but this award is really to be shared with all the crew who were out on the shout that day in very difficult conditions'.

Coxswain Daniel Potter recalls that the *Galasma* service was in the worst weather that he had experienced in 36 years with the RNLI. 'The sea just got bigger and bigger as we headed out to find the *Galasma* and I knew it was going to be one of the worst trips of my life. We were all relieved to get back home, wet but safe, and I kissed the bow of the boat at the end.'

Operations Director Michael Vlasto wrote to the station: 'This was a challenging and arduous service and the seamanship and teamwork demonstrated by Coxswain Potter and his crew were of the highest order. Please thank them all on my behalf. Well done, all of you!'

The other crewmen on the service were Bernie Davies, Tim Harrison, Ceri Knapgate and Peter Yates.

The 30ft yacht *Galasma* with five people aboard had lost all engine power in bad weather and a rough sea 20 miles off Aberystwyth. The New Quay boat was first on the scene, to be assisted later by the Pwllheli lifeboat. This dramatic photograph of *Galasma* and the Pwllheli lifeboat was taken from the *Frank and Lena Clifford of Stourbridge* by New Quay crew member Hanna Nuuttila and won the RNLI Photograph of the Year competition in 2008.

This photograph of *Frank and Lena Clifford of Stourbridge* in the relative shelter of New Quay Bay on her return from the shout to rescue *Galasma* gives some idea of what conditions must haven been like 20 miles out at sea.

More rough weather for *Frank and Lena Clifford of Stourbridge*, this time on exercise in New Quay Bay. Photograph by Joanna Jameson.

To get home safely,
he needs your support

I gyrraedd adref yn saff, mae
angen eich cefnogaeth arno

THE YEAR 2008 proved to be a busy one. The lifeboats were launched 29 times with 31 people being rescued. Ten of these services were made in darkness and five in weather conditions above Force 7. There was an unusual service on April 12 of that year. A BBC film crew was making a documentary reconstruction of an incident at Llangrannog the previous year.

After filming the launch of both lifeboats from the boathouse, the film crew proceeded to Llangrannog where *Frank and Lena Clifford of Stourbridge* was tasked to recover a stunt woman who was in the water playing the part of the original casualty.

The stunt woman was in distress and had already been put in a safety boat, and following an assessment by the lifeboat crew, the two boats returned to New Quay where the casualty was handed over to paramedics on the pier. She was suffering from hypothermia, shock and sea sickness and was taken to hospital. The plans for filming were abandoned, an ironic end to what was supposed to be a reconstruction of the 2007 rescue.

On May 5, 2008, the *Frank and Lena Clifford of Stourbridge* was launched to assist a 48ft dive support vessel *Wandering Star* taking on water and sinking two miles south of Cardigan Island. The vessel had been supporting the longboats taking part in the Celtic Challenge race, which had been abandoned because of bad weather in the Irish Sea. Coming alongside *Wandering Star*, the

Crew member Ceri Knapgate appeared in an RNLI fundraising advertising campaign in 2011. The picture was taken aboard the *Frank and Lena Clifford of Stourbridge* by lifeboat photographer Nigel Millard, whose coffee-table book of photographs The Lifeboat was published in 2013.

Albert Moller retired as Lifeboat Operations Manager in March 2009 having held the post for more than six years. Here he hands over to his successor, Roger Couch. From left: Simon Williams, Simon Rigby, Ceri Knapgate, Ben Billingham, Mervyn Thomas, Albert Moller, Daniel Potter, Roger Couch, Jolyon Quayle, Tim Harrison, Derek Roberts, Roger Colman.

lifeboat immediately deployed the salvage pump for 40 minutes before a lifeboatman from Cardigan effected a repair on board.

The ALB was launched at 10.30am on August 10 after a Mayday call to Milford Haven Coastguard from the yacht *Cadenza* with three people on board. The 26-foot yacht had lost her main mast and was in serious difficulties in the strong wind and rough sea. RFA *Mounts Bay*, anchored off New Quay for the Regatta, also heard the Mayday call and launched one of her RIBs which was unable to assist because of the wind and heavy seas. The lifeboats located the yacht two and a half miles north of New Quay and took her under tow to New Quay harbour at 11.30am.

Frank and Lena Clifford of Stourbridge left on passage to Conwy for attention to one of her engines and was replaced by relief boat ON-1187 *Mary Margaret*. The relief lifeboat and ILB *Amy Lea* were launched at 4pm on February 11, 2009, to an incident involving a paraglider who was base jumping near Cwmtydu. On reaching the scene, the lifeboats spotted some blue parachute silk at the bottom of the cliffs between the Old Coastguard Lookout and Cwmtydu. Rescue 169, a Sea King helicopter from RMB Chivenor, was also at the scene but unable to see the casualty.

With binoculars, the ALB crew located the casualty in bushes some 200 feet from the top of the 500ft high cliffs and directed the helicopter to the correct position using the VHF radio. The casualty was lifted off the cliff by the helicopter winch and taken to hospital with minor injuries. The ILB crew recovered the parachute pack from the bottom of the cliffs to be returned to the owner in due course.

The all weather lifeboat was called out on a difficult night rescue on September 10, 2009, to assist a 31-foot yacht, *Monkey Business 2* and its crew of two with intermittent engine trouble 27 miles west of New Quay.

Pressed into service by the Coastguard because of difficult sea conditions (a nasty swell and potentially strengthening Force 5 winds), the crew of seven led by coxswain Daniel Potter set out soon after 10 pm and, after locating the yacht around midnight, decided that crew members Rees-Tom Jones and Ceri Knapgate should be put on board to secure a tow rope.

The yacht was successfully towed to New Quay, arriving around 4am. Lifeboat Operations Manager Roger Couch said, 'The dedication of our crew was demonstrated by the speedy response to the call even though it meant an all night rescue. The operation went smoothly, and we were able to bring two very grateful sailors to the beach'.

Both relief lifeboats ALB *Lifetime Care* and the ILB were launched at 6.45am on September 29, 2009, to assist the 10-metre catamaran *Wild Goose 2* with two people on board just off the entrance to Aberaeron Harbour. On passage north, the catamaran had fouled her propeller and was in danger of going onto the rocks. The ILB reached the scene first and after a quick assessment of the situation, crew member Ceri Knapgate went into the water and cut the propeller free. *Wild Goose 2* was then able to get under way and resumed her passage north.

After every shout and exercise, the lifeboat, the tractor and carriage and all the launching gear is cleaned and everything prepared for the next call-out whenever that may be. Here the Talus tractor gets a clean-down at the boathouse at the end of an exercise. Photograph by Nigel Millard.

Courtesy of the RNLI

A dog fell off the cliffs north of Llangrannog on May 15, 2010, and *Amy Lea* was launched to help. She soon located the injured dog, Zoe, a two-year-old spaniel, which was taken on board and is pictured with crew member Gary Hartley on his first ILB shout on its way to Llangrannog to be united with its owner.

Courtesy of the RNLI

Amy Lea was called out on October 29, 2010, to assist a tender dinghy with two people on board just off New Quay Fish Factory unable to restart the engine. The lifeboat quickly found the dinghy and towed her to safety in the harbour. The picture shows helmsman Ben Billingham with the tender in tow behind the ILB.

Lerina, a scalloper with an injured man on board, ten miles off Aberporth in 2010. The helicopter could not lower the winchman onto the boat because of the mass of rigging. *Frank and Lena* went alongside and put the winchman on board, before the injured man and the winchman were transferred to the ALB

The lifeboat comes to the rescue of a local fishing-boat *Catherine Arden*, AB 67, a familiar and well-loved sight in New Quay Bay for more than 35 years from the 1970s. Here, a lobster pot had fouled the propellor and the boat was towed back to New Quay

Frank and Lena Clifford of Stourbridge cuts through the waves

during a bad weather exercise in 2009. Photograph by Emyr Rhys Williams.

Crewman Gary Hartley is winched aboard the Search and Rescue helicopter from ALB 12-15, *Frank and Lena Clifford of Stourbridge*, during an exercise. Picture by Ben Billingham

A CALL to help a fishing boat *Lerina* with an injured man on board nine miles west of New Quay developed into an eight-hour rescue for *Frank and Lena Clifford of Stourbridge* on March 3, 2010. On reaching the scalloping vessel, Coxswain Dan Potter manoeuvred the lifeboat in very difficult tidal conditions so that the crew could get aboard to give first aid to the injured man, who had suffered head and neck injuries. Sea King helicopter Rescue 122 from RAF Valley had been called but the winchman could not land on the boat because of the mass of rigging.

The lifeboat was again manoeuvred alongside and the injured man transferred to the after deck of the ALB. The winchman from the helicopter then lifted the casualty from the lifeboat and took him to Ysbyty Gwynedd, Bangor.

The lifeboat was then taken alongside the *Lerina* and two lifeboatmen put aboard to help the skipper lift his fishing gear and stow it ready to sail back to Fishguard. The gear had fouled the propeller and rudder, and a decision was made to tow the vessel south.

Both Cardigan lifeboats happened to be on exercise, and soon two divers arrived on the scene and quickly cleared the problem. The lifeboat returned to New Quay at 8.45pm having been at sea for eight hours.

Both lifeboats were launched at 5.25pm on July 28, 2010, to assist the *Maid Moira* with the two people on board aground on rocks between Llanon and Llanrhystud. The ILB was able to pull the yacht off the rocks; a tow was attached to the ALB and the yacht was towed to New Quay.

Nearer home, *Amy Lea* was launched on June 21, 2010, to assist a person in the water off Traethgwyn beach near Quay West holiday park. The lifeboat quickly located a 25-year-old female some 40 yards off shore who was taken on to the boat and given first aid and oxygen by the crew. She was landed on the quay at New Quay and taken to Bronglais Hospital, Aberystwyth.

The year 2011 proved to be an extremely busy one for the inshore lifeboat and one of the first services by the relief ILB D-690 *David Young* was on March 26, 2011, to assist families trapped by the incoming tide on rocks south of the lifeboat station,

Eleven people – seven adults and four children, including a baby in a buggy – were taken off and landed safely ashore. The official narrative proudly reports: 'The child in the baby buggy was not disturbed, having been loaded on and off the lifeboat without being wakened'. The crew were Ben Billingham, Bernie Davies and Simon Rigby.

Amy Lea was launched twice on June 14, saving a life on each shout. First, the ILB had rescued from the water, a 'despondent male' who jumped off cliffs near Aberaeron, giving him first aid before taking him to Aberaeron. Later in the day, two kayakers were in difficulty and had been in the water for some time. The crew took them onto the lifeboat and administered first aid, landing them on the pier to be taken to hospital by ambulance.

A dramatic photo taken from the *Amy Lea* inshore boat during a helicopter and lifeboat exercise in New Quay Bay, with New Quay Head and Target Rock in the background. The RAF Rescue Sea King helicopter based at Chivenor, Devon, has been involved in a number of real-life rescues with the *Frank and Lena Clifford of Stourbridge*.

Rescue on the rocks at Ynys Lochtyn

The station has been involved in a good number of courageous and dramatic and life-saving rescues. One of the more recent took place in 2011, for which four New Quay lifeboatmen were honoured in 2012 for rescuing a 70-year-old angler who sustained serious head injuries, broken ribs and a collapsed lung after falling on to rocks at Ynys Lochtyn, Llangrannog.

The highest accolade was awarded to Gary Hartley, who received a Certificate for Exceptional First Aid to a Casualty, the first RNLI volunteer in Wales to be presented with the honour, and only the eighth time across the UK that the award has been made. This award is exceptionally bestowed and awarded by the RNLI in circumstances where lives are saved under the most difficult of conditions.

Tim Harrison received a Letter of Commendation and Thanks, signed by Prof Charles Deakin, chairman of the medical and survival committee of the RNLI. Simon Rigby and Bernard Davies both received Letters of Thanks signed by Paul Boissier, chief executive of the RNLI.

The rescue started when crew member Tim Harrison, who happened to be in Llangrannog, alerted the Coastguard who then phoned the Lifeboat Station. Lifeboat Operations Manager Roger Couch had just put down the phone on that call when Tim Harrison rang in, saying he was giving assistance to a badly injured man on the rocks and that the tide was coming in very quickly. He requested first-aiders and the station scoop stretcher. These were quickly requisitioned and proved crucial in saving the man's life.

This is a verbatim account of the Station's official report: 'On September 27, 2011, the RNLI inshore lifeboat *Amy Lea*, was called out at 6pm. The volunteer crew, with Bernard Davies at the helm, made haste to the scene. It was obvious that the man was in a serious condition and on arrival, RNLI volunteer Gary Hartley immediately administered oxygen and first aid having assessed the man's condition. The lifeboat crew then prepared the casualty for evacuation from the shoreline due to the tide rising rapidly around them.

The injured man was transferred by scoop stretcher to the RNLI lifeboat, where Gary continued to give first-aid whilst the lifeboat moved clear of the shoreline. The RAF rescue helicopter Rescue 169 had arrived from Chivenor and the paramedic was lowered to the inshore lifeboat but the casualty was in too poor a condition to be winched up. The helicopter was instead requested to land on Llangrannog beach, where the lifeboat was beached, and the casualty carefully transferred to the aircraft. He was then airlifted to Withybush Hospital where he underwent a long period of treatment'.

The crewmen involved in the Ynys Lochtyn rescue with their awards presented in the lifeboat station by Colin Williams, RNLI divisional inspector of lifeboats for Wales and the Isle of Man. He praised the crew's excellent teamwork in an extremely challenging situation. From the left: Colin Williams, Tim Harrison, Simon Rigby, Gary Hartley, Bernie Davies and Lifeboat Operations Manager Roger Couch.

A dramatic life-saving rescue at Cwmtydu in 2012. Bernie Davies offers an outstretched hand to transfer a very weak swimmer who had been rescued by the ILB *Amy Lea* on to *Frank and Lena Clifford of Stourbridge*. Ceri Knapgate is at the helm in the ILB and the other crew members were Simon Rigby and Elis Jones. Daniel Potter was Coxswain of the ALB. Both crews received a Letter of Thanks for their part in the rescue. Picture: RNLI

On the opposite page, RAF Valley Search and Rescue Sea King helicopter 122 winches the casualty from the *Frank and Lena Clifford of Stourbridge* to the helicopter. Prince William was based at RAF Valley at the time as a helicopter pilot. Picture by Morlais Davies

CREWS of both the all weather lifeboat and the inshore boat received a Letter of Thanks for their part in a dramatic life-saving rescue of a man who had been swept out to sea at Cwmtydu on August 30, 2012.

Both boats had been called out shortly before 4.15pm after a report of a lone swimmer in the water in 'extreme difficulty'.

Battling heavy seas and a Force 7 near gale, the boats found the casualty suffering from hypothermia having been in the water for more than half an hour. The man was lifted into the ILB before being helped onto the ALB for first aid attention on the way back to New Quay. (See pictures on preceding pages).

The RAF helicopter from Valley on Anglesey could not pick up the casualty at first because of the stormy conditions and eventually the casuality was winched up to the helicopter from the ALB, which had moved to a sheltered position in New Quay harbour.

Daniel Potter was Coxswain of the ALB and Ceri Knapgate at the helm of the ILB. In his letter to the station, Operations Director Michael Vlasto said: 'Both crews demonstrated excellent teamwork, initiative and communications under difficult conditions. I commend the commitment and professionalism of all involved in achieving a positive outcome.'

Lifeboat Operations Manager Roger Couch said: 'Our volunteer crews are extremely dedicated and this sort of commendation is only given for exceptional service'.

The Team 2014

Top row (from left): **Roger Couch** Lifeboat Operations Manager. **Roger Davies** Deputy Launching Authority. **Vince Thomas** Deputy Launching Authority. **Daniel Potter** Coxswain/Second Mechanic. **Steve Hartley** Second Coxswain. **Ben Billingham** Station Mechanic.

Row 2: **Rees-Tom Jones** Deputy Second Coxswain. **Tim Harrison** Deputy Second Coxswain/ILB Helmsman. **Bernie Davies** ALB Crew/ILB Senior Helmsman/Third Mechanic. **Brett Stones** ALB Crew/ILB Senior Helmsman. **Simon Rigby** ALB Crew/ILB Helmsman. **Peter Yates** ALB Crew/ILB Helmsman.

Row 3: **Hefin Davies** ALB/ILB Crew. **Tomas Davies** ALB/ILB Crew. **Sarah Perry** ALB/ILB Crew. **Joe Quayle** ALB/ILB Crew/Emergency Mechanic. **Dylan Price** ALB/ILB Crew/Tractor Driver. **Mike Evans** ALB/ILB Crew.

Row 4: **Laura Mears** ALB/ILB Crew. **Craig Miller** ALB/ILB Crew. **Tom Evans** ALB/ILB Crew. **Trevor Evans** Emergency DLA/Shore Crew. **Dai Price** Senior Tractor Driver/Shore Crew. **Mick Jennings** Tractor Driver/Shore Crew.

Bottom Row: **Roger Colman** Shore Crew. **Gareth Tanner** Shore Crew. **Sally Greene** Shore Crew. **Bill Liston** Shore Crew. **Gregg Evitts** Shore Crew. **John Simpson** Shore Crew.

Other station officials: **Dr Leo O'Connor** Medical Advisor. **Dr Rob Morgan** Deputy Medical Advisor. **Pete Kemp** Treasurer. **Glyn Griffiths** Press Officer. **Roy Fenner** Safety Officer. **The Rev. Matthew Baynham** Chaplain.

Picture montage by Morlais Davies

127

New Quay's new inshore lifeboat *D-754 Audrey LJ* was called into action on September 17, 2012, less than a week after entering service. A cruiser was in difficulties just north of Aberaeron harbour and *Frank and Lena Clifford of Stourbridge* was launched at 7.30pm. The *Audrey LJ* was launched soon after.

There was a heavy swell and conditions were difficult; Mechanic Ben Billingham was transferred from the ALB on to the stricken vessel to set up a tow. 'Once the tow was established, the casualty's anchor was cut away as it couldn't be recovered. Bernie Davies of the *Audrey LJ* was put on board'.

The boat was then skilfully manoeuvred into Aberaeron harbour which was made difficult because of the swell and failing light.

The first shout in 2014 was very early in the year - January 4. At 10.50pm, *Audrey LJ* was called out after a report of a 'despondent' young man on the rocks at the end of the pier in very bad weather and a very high Spring tide. The boat stood by near the scene as Coastguards and police took up positions on the landwardside and persuaded the man to get back on the pier.

The Lifeboat at New Quay has suffered a great loss in the last few years with four stalwarts of the RNLI dying within a short time. Arnold Thomas, Hon Sec from 1980 to 1984, died in January 2010, and Albert Moller, Lifeboat Operations Manager from 2003 until 2009, died a year later.

The town was saddened in March 2012 by the sudden death of Mervyn Thomas, one of the longest serving members at New Quay. He joined the crew as a volunteer in 1967 aged 17 and served as Station Mechanic for 26 years from 1975 to 2001. Later he took on the important role of Deputy Launching Authority. During his career, he received the Bronze Medal for a dramatic rescue at Trwyn Crou (see page 64) and Thanks Inscribed on Vellum for his key role in the rescue of Up Spirits (see page 66).

Shortly before his death, he was awarded an Inscribed Statuette in acknowledgement of his long service and contribution to saving lives at sea. The statuette was presented to Mervyn's widow Anne at the naming ceremony of the Audrey LJ in October 2012. His family asked mourners to donate money to the lifeboat station in lieu of flowers at his funeral. More than £1,000 was raised. The family connection with the Lifeboat is maintained by Mervyn's brother Vince, who is a Deputy Launching Authority at the Station.

In October that year, another New Quay lifeboat stalwart died. Dennis Leworthy served as a crew member from 1943 to 1952 and as a shore crew member until 1980. After retiring from the Coastguard, he became the New Quay Harbourmaster, and also a Deputy Launching Authority at the station. In 1984 he was appointed Hon Sec, a post he held until 1996. In a fitting tribute to his work, the four bearers of the coffin at his funeral were long-serving New Quay lifeboat men, Daniel Potter, Rees-Tom Jones, Bernard Davies and Steve Hartley.

RNLI Lifeguards now patrol more than 200 beaches in the UK and the Channel Islands, responding to 14,519 incidents in 2012. The Ceredigion RNLI Lifeguards are pictured here at Llangrannog in June, 2013. Two Lifeguards are on duty at New Quay from June to July and three during the school holidays. Lifeguards are qualified in lifesaving and casualty care, but most of their work is prevention – monitoring sea conditions and watching people on the beach.

HM Coastguard

Her Majesty's Coastguard has a long and proud history, owing its origins to efforts made to combat smuggling in the 17th and 18th centuries. Late in the 18th century, the service was expanded to include the use of Naval vessels, Revenue cruisers and a land-based mounted force called Riding Officers, who had patrolled the shore since 1698. In 1809, the Preventative Water Guard was established, its primary objective to prevent smuggling in coastal waters, but also to give assistance to shipwrecks and take some responsibility for life saving.

In New Quay, the Revenue Watch House (now The Old Watch House restaurant) was built a year later in 1810 above Penwig reef. Apart from being an excellent vantage point for surveying the bay, it provided living quarters for the Chief Coastguard and his family.

His Majesty's Coastguard Service was officially established in 1822 when the Preventative Water Guard, the Revenue cruisers and the Riding Officers were amalgamated in a crack-down on smuggling. Later they were given responsibility for saving lives as well.

For security reasons to prevent collusion with smugglers, Coastguards were not allowed to be local men, but many of them who did service in New Quay, remained in the town after they retired.

Today Her Majesty's Coastguard is responsible for the initiation and co-ordination of all civilian maritime search and rescue. This includes the mobilisation, organisation and tasking of adequate resources to respond to persons either in distress at sea, or to persons at risk of injury or death on the cliffs or shoreline of the UK.

The auxiliary station at New Quay operates under the aegis of the regional Maritime Rescue Co-ordination Centre at Milford Haven. Station Officer is Lyn Davies and he has a team of ten volunteers. HM Coastguard works closely with the RNLI and RAF Squadron 22, the search and rescue service at RAF Valley and Royal Marines Base, Chivenor, Devon, for rescues at sea.

Call-outs are extremely varied. In August 2003, the Coastguard got a call at 11.30pm that six people were stranded on a ledge on the cliffs near the Drewi waterfall north of New Quay. It was late, dark and high tide, and so the six casualties were lowered slowly and safely one by one by the Cliff Rescue Team down the cliff and onto the waiting inshore lifeboat. This was a very satisfactory rescue, completed at 2.45am.

The following year, New Quay Coastguard was called out to a very different type of incident: a large bottle-nosed dolphin stranded at Ynys Lochtyn, Llangrannnog. It was the Coastguards' job to throw buckets of sea water over the mammal to keep it alive.

After more than eight hours of this, and waiting for the tide to run, the rescuers successfully managed to support the mammal on both sides and refloat it. There were great cheers when it swam out to sea.

New Quay Coastguards 2014. Clockwise from front left: Mike Hallam, Lyn Davies, Brian Davies, Gerwyn Williams. Right, from front: Elfyn Davies (universally known as Knox), Bleddyn Evans, Alun Davies, Jeff Davies, Mark Evans.

RNLI Chief Executive Paul Boissier visited New Quay Lifeboat Station on June 6, 2013. He was given a tour of the station and the Cambrian News reported that he 'commented favourably on its location, appearance and the standard of the two lifeboats'.

A young holidaymaker dislocated his hip while on his grandfather's boat in New Quay Harbour on July 27, 2013 and the *Audrey LJ* ILB was launched to go to his aid.

Ceredigion RNLI LIfeguard Heather Llewelyn was already giving assistance when the ILB arrived. The three-man crew was quick to administer first aid and pain relief to nine-year-old Ethan Read, from Hereford, who was carefully lifted on to a stretcher and transferred to the ILB and then to the beach to await an ambulance to take him to hospital, where he had an emergency operation at midnight.

The Crew members involved were so impressed with Ethan's bravery that they visited him a few days later in Bronglais Hospital, Aberystwyth. Pictured (clockwise from left:) RNLI lifeguard Heather Llewelyn, New Quay Lifeboatmen Bernie Davies, Simon Rigby, and Ben Billingham with Ethan.

Ethan's grandmother Lynda Read wrote a letter to the station: 'I thank you all for the wonderful help you gave to Ethan'.

Later she added: 'Ethan's dad is so impressed with all the team he cannot get over the fact the RNLI crews not only gave up their time to do the job as a volunteer but also gave up an evening to come and visit a little lad. Pure class!'

Crew members proudly display their Queen's Diamond Jubilee Medals presented to them at the naming ceremony of the *Audrey LJ* in September 2012. Trevor Evans (left) and Rees-Tom Jones (third left) also received bars to their long-service badges. In the centre of the picture, Anne, the widow of Mervyn Thomas, proudly holds his medal and Inscribed Statuette. Sara Edwards, Deputy Lord Lieutenant of Dyfed, presented the awards and stands next to the Lifeboat Operations Manager Roger Couch

134

Fund-raisers

FUNDRAISERS have been an essential and much-valued part of the RNLI family for more than 150 years. And they still are. Collectors come in all shapes and sizes and ages, but none surely much smaller and younger than this little girl: two-year-old Brenda Avril Fish collecting on lifeboat day at New Quay in 1934.

This enchanting picture, featured in The Lifeboat, the journal of the RNLI, was taken by her father, James Henry Fish, engineer on the Alpha, the fisheries protection vessel based at New Quay, and a member of the lifeboat crew. The picture was taken outside the house where she lived, The Cliffe, on Glanmor Terrace, appropriately just opposite the steep lane down to the lifeboat station. She later studied geography and geology at the University College of Wales, Aberystwyth, and became a teacher, marrying Russell Cooper She now lives in Abergavenny.

Historically, fundraising in New Quay involved the whole community and was vital in keeping the lifeboat on station. Today there is a different demographic, and the branch relies on the generosity of local businesses and holidaymakers.

Lis Singer, branch fundraising chair, says: 'New Quay is unique in that the traditional families live on – houses are owned by the descendants of the original families and grandchildren and great-grandchildren are still very much part of the community if only during school holidays. This young generation is vital for the future'.

Courtesy of the RNLI

By courtesy of]   *[Mr. J. H. Fish, New Quay, Cardiganshire.*
AGED TWO.
Miss Brenda Avril Fish collecting on life-boat day at New Quay, Cardigan.

St Albans RNLI

Members of the St Albans and District Branch of the RNLI on a visit to Southend on Sea Lifeboat Station in 2012.

The Branch is proud of its history of fundraising, not only in raising the money to pay for a lifeboat, St Albans, in the branch's jubilee year, but also, for instance, helping to raise money to buy a Spitfire during the Second World War.

Stourbridge RNLI fundraisers at work in 2011. Sue Coombes, Hon Sec, is third left and Chris Fonteyn, Chairman, fourth left

Stourbridge RNLI

The Stourbridge Branch of the RNLI has been a very active fundraising group for more than 100 years. Fundraising events have included bucket and street collections, coffee mornings and such, and an annual Sponsored Knit-In organised by Pam Grice that ran for 32 years, raised more than £30,000.

The highlight of the fundraising year in 2013 was a Zumbathon, which raised more than £2,000 and which was restricted to New Quay Lifeboat Station. LOM Roger Couch said: 'What a wonderful total and thank you so much'.

Fundraising members of the New Quay branch of the RNLI at the Christmas Fayre at the Penwig Hotel in 2013. Father Christmas arrived at the quay by inshore lifeboat, children from New Quay Primary School sang carols outside the hotel and people packed around the stalls inside. A very enjoyable – and profitable – morning. Photograph by Jem Moore.

Inset: a photograph of the Ladies' Lifeboat Guild outside the Penwig in 2000.

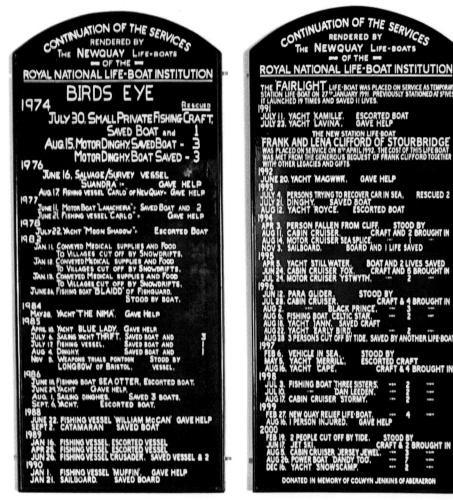

Three of the service boards in the boathouse listing shouts from 1974 until 2009.

Services Rendered

Service boards at the lifeboat station list the number of effective services the lifeboats have made.

The board on the right was sign-written in February 2014 and brings the services of the New Quay all weather boat up to date.

The entries on the service boards are all the rescues/shouts/services that RNLI Poole judges to be effective services.

At the end of the book, there is a comprehensive list of all the services from the New Quay Lifeboat station from 1864. The earlier pulling and sailing boats and then the all weather boats have been launched on 394 occasions.

The inshore lifeboat, which came on station in 1967, has been launched 545 times and rescued 530 people.

The list was compiled from a number of sources and has been very slightly edited stylewise to smooth things out. Compilation of the data at the RNLI has changed over the last 150 years

Before 1970, a person rescued was counted as a life saved, therefore the total number of lives saved pre-1970 is the same as the number of people rescued. From 1970 onwards, they were counted separately.

Later, annual statistics were kept of the number of times the lifeboat was launched but not adjudged to have effected a service.

This poem in Welsh was written by Calvin Griffiths, a work colleague of long-serving New Quay lifeboatman Rees-Tom Jones. Over the years Rees-Tom had regaled his friend with stories from the lifeboat. They made such an impression that Calvin wrote this poem specially for the New Quay Lifeboat in 2009.

Bâd Achub

Ar frig y don ym merw'r môr
mewn niwl ar nos yn fagddu,
dim taw i'r ysgwyd, gwynt na'r glaw
dibynnwn ar y weddi.

Nid ofer troelli'r moroedd mawr,
achubwyd ef rhag boddi
a'i falhder mwy na'n balchder ni
cael ateb wnaeth i'w weddi.

Mihangel

RNLI

On the crest of the wave in the seething sea
In fog and the night pitch black,
No end to the swaying, wind and rain
We put our faith in prayer.

Not in vain did we ride the great seas,
He was saved from drowning
And his joy far greater than ours.
His prayer was answered.

The Future

The Mersey Class all weather lifeboats have a planned life of 25 years and are being replaced by the RNLI's new fast carriage boat, the Shannon Class.

With a top speed of 25 knots, the new boat is 50 per cent faster than the Mersey, and is jet-propelled, using water jet propulsion, which gives the Shannon extraordinary manoeuvrability

It can turn on a proverbial sixpence, and effectively has brakes: its stopping speed from 25 knots to zero is 3 seconds.

The twin water jets also mean the Shannon will be able to operate in shallow water and reduces the risk of damage during launch and recovery and when intentionally beached

The new boat is powered by two 650hp Scania 13-litre turbodiesel engines and propelled by two Hamilton HJ Waterjets. A measure of how technology has moved on is that the first motor lifeboat at New Quay, the *St Albans*, was powered by two 18hp engines. In 1948, that was seen, rightly, as a great advance.

The RNLI hopes to build 50 in the next ten years, predicting that they will rescue more than 56,000 people.

The Shannon will be the first class of lifeboat to be built in-house at the new all-weather lifeboat centre at RNLI HQ at Poole.

This photograph was taken by Joanna Jameson at New Quay when the Shannon lifeboat made a visit in 2013.

Services of the New Quay Lifeboat (ALB)

Forester

1870	Feb 14	A barge, saved abandoned barge

Nelson

1872	Oct 16	Ship ANTIGUA, of Greenock, rendered assistance & stood by
1880	Jan 1	Barque PACIFIC, of Swansea, rendered assistance
1884	Nov 21	Brigantine ALBERT, of Carlisle, saved vessel and 5

Frank and Marion

1887	May 20	Schooner INDUSTRY, of Aberystwyth, saved 4
1900	Nov 7	Dandy ANN ELIZA, of Cardigan, saved 3
	Nov 12	Fishing boat RANGER, of New Quay, saved 3
1903	Sept 10	Ketch ISABEL, of Milford, landed 7. Assisted to save vessel
	Dec 8	Ketch TELEPHONE, of Padstow, saved vessel and 2
1906	Nov 19	Schooner TWO BROTHERS, of Carnarvon, saved vessel and 4
	Nov 19	and Ketch LEANDER, of Carnarvon, saved 3

William Cantrell Ashley

1915	July 16	Fishing boat WHITE ROSE, of New Quay, saved boat and 2
1916	Nov 3	Fishing boat GWEN, of New Quay, assisted to save boat
1917	Aug 22	Punt ALBERT, of New Quay, saved 2

	Aug 22	Fishing boat DANIEL AND JANE, of New Quay, saved 2
1920	Nov 16	Obsolete cruiser AMETHYST, landed 7
1924	July 3	Fishing boat WINIFREIDA, of Aberayron, saved 2
1930	Mar 20	Fishing boat ROSE, of New Quay, stood by
1938	May 31	Fishing boat PEGGY, of New Quay, escorted to harbour
1939	June 28	Sailing dinghy IDLE HOUR, of New Quay, saved dinghy and 2
1946	Feb 5	H.M.Submarine UNIVERSAL, stood by
1947	Oct 21	Motor fishing boat SEABREEZE, of Aberayron, gave help

St Albans

1950	July 31	Motor boat KITTIWAKE, of Aberayron, saved boat & 1
	Aug 11	Motor boat HALLOWEEN, of New Quay, saved boat &14
1951	Aug 18	Fishing boat CA.5, of Aberaeron, saved boat & 3
	Aug 31	Man over cliff, landed 2 and a body
1952	Feb 10	Man over cliff, landed a body
1955	July 17	Anglers marooned on rocks, saved 10
1956	Aug 23	Yacht RONSAY, of Aberayron, escorted
	Sept 15	Fishing fleet, of New Quay, escorted fleet. Landed 2
1957	Apr 17	Fishing boat CAMELIA, escorted
	June 27	Fishing boat DOLIUS, saved boat and 2
1958	July 13	Fishing boat YNYS LOCHTYN, escorted
1960	Aug 21	Yacht SYLVIA, escorted, landed 5
1961	Aug 5	Four racing yachts, saved 4 yachts and 12

	Aug 14	Fishing boat GWYLAN, saved boat and 3
1962	June 1	Boy over cliff, saved 1
	Aug 14	Two inflatable dinghies, saved dinghies and 2
	Aug 14	Yacht ARK, saved yacht and 2
1963	July 19	Rowing boat GWYLAN II, saved boat and 3
1964	July 7	Motor boat GWYLAN, saved boat and 1
1965	June 7	Fishing boat ROSALINE, saved boat and 2
	Aug 4	Three yachts, escorted one yacht, saved two yachts and 6
	Sept 8	Lobster fishing boat, escorted
1966	May 22	Yacht SEAJAY, gave help
	Aug 4	Motor launch SULLY QUEEN, saved launch and 3
	Aug 7	Three boys over cliff, saved 1 and landed 2 bodies
	Sept 3	Yacht BERCEUSE, escorted
	Sept 3	Small boat, escorted
	Oct 1	Fishing boats SEA BREEZE, TORBAY LASS, KINGFISHER and MARY ARDEN, and yacht TIC TAC, escorted
1967	June 20	Yacht TIC TAC, saved yacht and 2
	June 28	Speedboat BLUE STAR, saved boat and recovered a body
	Aug 16	Man over cliff, landed 3 and a body
	Aug 16	Catamaran in tow of fishing boat, escorted
	Sept 2	Motor yacht PANDORA, saved yacht and 5
1968	Apr 14	Man over cliff, landed injured man
	Aug 29	Yacht MO-JO, saved yacht and 4
	Sept 12	Fishing boat TORBAY LASS, gave help
1970	May 13	Motor fishing boat VIGILANT, gave help
	June 19	Converted Lifeboat WYORA, gave help

Birds Eye

1971	Aug 10	Fishing boat FREEBOOTER, saved boat and 3
	Aug 28	Yacht SMARTIE, saved yacht and 2
	Sept 19	Fishing boat EVE, gave help
	Oct 23	Cabin cruiser NEREUS BAHAMAS, saved 3
1972	Apr 17	Gave help for a stranded cliff climber
	July 9	Fishing boat DERSONJA, escorted
	Aug 7	Assisted to save 2 boys stranded on a cliff, 2
	Oct 2	Fishing boat ENDEAVOUR I, gave help
1973	Aug 1	Inflatable dinghy, escorted
	Aug 6	Yachts CORNFLOWER, SAMEEN, MYFANWY and
		SARAH, saved yachts and 12
	Aug 12	Dinghy, saved dinghy and 2
	Aug 26	Stood by for person cut off by tide
	Sept 19	Yacht SUSIE WONG saved yacht and 3
1974	Apr 28	Motor cruiser JEB, saved cruiser and 2
	July 30	Fishing boat, saved boat and 1
	Aug 15	Motor dinghy, saved dinghy and 3
1976	June 16	Salvage vessel SUANDRA, gave help
	Aug 17	Fishing boat CARLO, gave help
1977	June 11	Motor launch LANACHEIRA, saved launch and 3
	June 21	Fishing boat CARLO, gave help
1978	July 22	Yacht MOON SHADOW, escorted
1982	Jan 11	Conveyed medical supplies and food to villages cut off by snowdrifts

	Jan 12	Conveyed medical supplies and food to villages cut off by snowdrifts
	Jan 13	Conveyed medical supplies and food to villages cut off by snowdrifts
	June 24	Fishing boat BLAIDD of Fishguard. Stood by boat.
1984	May 28	Yacht THE NIMA, gave help
1985	Apr 16	Yacht BLUE LADY, gave help
	July 6	Sailing yacht THRIFT, saved boat and 3
	July 12	Fishing vessel, saved boat and 1
	Aug 4	Dinghy, saved boat and 1
	Nov 5	Weapon trials pontoon LONGBOW of Bristol. Stood by vessel
1986	June 18	Fishing boat SEA OTTER, escorted boat
	June 29	Yacht, gave help
	Aug 1	Sailing dinghies, saved 3 boats
	Sept 6	Yacht, escorted boat
1988	June 22	Fishing vessel WILLIAM McCAN, gave help
	Sept 2	Catamaran, saved boat
1989	Jan 16	Fishing vessel, escorted vessel
	Apr 25	Fishing vessel, escorted vessel
	June 26	Fishing vessel. CRUSADER saved vessel and 2
1990	Jan 1	Fishing vessel MUFFIN, gave help
	Jan 21	Sailboard, saved board
1991	July 11	Yacht KAMILLE, escorted boat. (RNLB Fairlight)
	July 23	Yacht LAVINA, gave help. (RNLB Fairlight)

Frank and Lena Clifford of Stourbridge

1992	June 20	Yacht MAGWR, gave help
1993	July 4	Persons trying to recover car in sea. Rescued 2
	July 21	Dinghy, saved boat
	Aug 12	Yacht ROYCE, escorted boat
1994	Apr 3	Person fallen from cliff. Stood by
	Aug 11	Cabin cruiser. Two persons and craft brought in
	Aug 14	Motor cruiser SEA SPLICE. One person and craft brought in
	Nov 3	Sailboard, one life and board saved
		Additionally, the lifeboat launched on a further 2 occasions
1995	Apr 5	Yacht STILL WATER. Two lives and boat saved
	June 24	Cabin cruiser FOX. Five persons and craft brought in
	July 24	Motor cruiser YSTWYTH. Two persons and craft brought in
		Additionally, the lifeboat launched on a further 6 occasions
1996	June 12	Para glider. Stood by
	July 28	Cabin cruiser. Four persons and craft brought
	Aug 2	Cabin cruiser BLACK PRINCE. 3 persons & craft brought in
	Aug 6	Fishing vessel CELTIC STAR. 2 persons & craft brought in
	Aug 18	Yacht IANN. Saved craft
	Aug 22	Yacht EARLY BIRD. Two persons and craft brought in
	Aug 28	3 persons cut off by tide. Saved by another lifeboat
		Additionally, the lifeboat launched on a further 5 occasions
1997	Feb 6	Motor vehicle in sea. Stood by
	May 5	Yacht MERRILL, escorted craft

	Aug 16	Yacht CAPE. Craft and four brought in
		Additionally, the lifeboat launched on a further 3 occasions
1998	July 3	Fishing vessel THREE SISTERS. 2 people landed & craft brought in
	July 10	Fishing vessel DAN LEEDEN. Two people and craft brought in
	Aug 17	Cabin cruiser STORMY. Two people and craft brought in
		Additionally, the lifeboat launched on a further 4 occasions
1999	Feb 27	New Quay relief ILB D-387. Four people and craft brought in
	Aug 16	One person injured, gave help
		Additionally, the lifeboat launched on a further 4 occasions
2000	Feb 19	Two people cut off by the tide, stood by
	June 17	Jet ski. Two people and craft brought in
	Aug 5	Cabin cruiser JERSEY JEWEL. 3 people and craft brought in
	Aug 26	Powerboat DANDY TOO. Seven people and craft brought in
	Dec 16	Yacht SNOWSCAMP. Craft and 2 brought in
		Additionally, the lifeboat launched on a further 3 occasions
2001	July 23	14 people cut off by the tide. 14 saved by another lifeboat
	Aug 14	Fishing vessel EVE MARIE, injured man. 1 person brought in
	Aug 31	Angler cut off by tide, stood by
		Additionally, the lifeboat launched on a further 1 occasion
2002	Apr 20	Yacht BLUEBIRD. Two people landed and craft brought in
		Additionally, the lifeboat launched on a further 1 occasion
2003	July 19	Cabin cruiser TEYMAR, gave help
	Aug 5	Speed boat KNOCKOUT. Craft and 1 brought in
	Aug 5	People stranded. 6 brought in

	Aug 29	People in sea, gave help
	Sept 1	Person in sea, gave help
		Additionally, the lifeboat launched on a further 4 occasions
2004	Aug 20	Powerboat WHISTLER, escorted craft
	Aug 30	Yacht COQUETTE. Craft and 6 brought in
		Additionally, the lifeboat launched on a further 3 occasions
2005	May 29	Kayak, escorted craft
	June 20	Power boat, craft and 2 brought in
	July 3	Passenger vessel ERMOL 6. Craft and 23 brought in
		Additionally, the lifeboat launched on a further 3 occasions
2006	May 29	Catamaran ODIN'S TREASURE, stood by, others coped
	July 22	Powered boat AQUILLA. Two people and craft brought in
	Aug 25	Canoes, gave help
	Oct 12	Fishing vessel KIRSTY ANN. Two people and craft brought in
		Additionally, the lifeboat launched on a further 6 occasions
2007	Apr 15	Powered boat C.J. Two people and craft brought in
	Apr 25	Human body. gave help
	Aug 21	Person in the sea. Gave help - administered First Aid
	Aug 26	Powered boat SEA WARRIOR. 7 people & craft brought in
	Sept 24	Person in the sea, gave help
		Additionally, the lifeboat launched on a further 6 occasions
2008	Jan 28	Fishing vessel FLOWING TIDE II. 3 people & craft brought in
	Mar 10	Sailboard. Sailboard brought in
	Mar 10	Canoe. Craft brought in
	Apr 2	Fishing vessel. Two people and craft brought in

	Apr 12	Sick woman on board powered boat. One person landed
	May 5	Dive support craft WANDERING STAR. Craft and 4 lives saved
	Aug 10	Yacht CADENZA. Three people landed and craft brought in
	Aug 15	Yacht CERIDWEN. Two people and craft brought in
	Aug 24	Yacht BLUE MOON. Two people landed craft brought in
	Sept 6	Yacht GALASMA. Five lives and craft saved
	Sept 8	Powered boat RAZZLE. Two people and craft brought in
	Sept 22	Powered boat CRAZY GECKO. Two people and craft brought in
		Additionally, the lifeboat launched on a further 5 occasions
2009	Feb 11	Person on cliff, stood by
	May 16	People in the sea. One life saved
	July 23	Fishing vessel CATHERINE ARDEN. 3 people, craft brought in
	Aug 18	Powered boat SHIYA. Gave help - released the tension
	Aug 18	Windsurfer, escorted craft
	Sept 9	Yacht MONKEY BUSINESS 2. Two people and craft brought in
	Oct 1	Fishing vessel ANNA LOUISE. 1 person and craft brought in
	Oct 8	Fishing vessel KIRSTY ANN. 3 people & craft brought in
		Additionally, the lifeboat launched on a further 6 occasions
2010	Mar 3	Fishing vessel LERINA, injured man. Assisted to save a life
	June 18	Yacht KISMIT. 2 people and craft brought in
	July 25	Catamaran KANOLAO 2 people and craft brought in
	July 28	Yacht MAID MOIRA. 2 people and craft brought in
	Aug18	Fishing vessel CATHERINE ARDEN. 2 people, craft brought in
	Oct 8	Catamaran OCEAN PROWLER. 2 people and craft brought in
		Additionally, the lifeboat launched on a further 3 occasions
2011	Jan 24	Fishing vessel GRATITUDE. 3 people and craft brought in

		Additionally, the lifeboat launched on a further 5 occasions
2012	Aug 11	Yacht MISSFIT dismasted, escorted into harbour.
	Aug 30	Person in water. One life saved
	Sept 16	Powered boat SUMMER WINE. Craft and persons towed to Aberaeron
	Dec 10	Fishing vessel SANDERLING taking on water, gave help
	Dec 13	Fishing vessel PIONEER. Towed to New Quay
		Additionally, the lifeboat launched on a further 5 occasions
2013	Apr 3	Yacht DAVICO. Craft and person towed to Aberystwyth.
	May 28	ILB, assistance given
	July 18	Yacht TOM BOMBADIL. Craft and crew towed to Aberystwyth
	July 22	Pleasure craft, assistance given
	July 22	Rowing boat, assistance given
		Additionally, the lifeboat launched on a further 2 occasions

Hon Secs

1864 Mr Arthur Hood, CO CG	1971 Capt Cosmo Jones
1868 Mr James Barry, CO CG.	1978 Mr Fred Cooper
1871 Mr Thomas Evans	1980 Mr Arnold Thomas
1872 Rev James Griffiths	1984 Mr Dennis Leworthy
1873 Mr Michael Fitzpatrick CO CG	1996 Mr Roger Davies
1875 Capt Thomas Jones	Lifeboat Operations Manager (LOM)
1881 Capt David James	Replaced title of Hon Sec in 2003
1890 Capt David Rees	2003 Mr Albert Moller
1937 Mr Brinley Rees	2009 Mr Roger Couch
1954 Capt Byron Jones	

Services of the New Quay Lifeboat (ILB)

D-122

1967	June 28	Speedboat, gave help
	Aug 12	Bathers, landed a body and saved 1
1968	May 12	Speedboats SEA MISS and LL037 saved two boats and 4
	May 19	Motor fishing vessel MORNING STAR, gave help
	Aug 29	Recovered a body from the sea
	Aug 29	Yacht MO-JO, saved yacht and landed 11
	Sept 11	Yacht, gave help
	Sept 12	Trawler TORBAY LASS, stood by
1969	Aug 15	Canoe, landed 1, saved canoe
	Sept 1	Yacht BIRDCHIMMER, saved 3
1970	July 31	Boy trapped on rocks, gave help
	Aug 14	Speedboat SATAN V, escorted
	Sept 13	Three sailing dinghies, landed 6
1971	May 29	Man fallen from cliff, landed injured man, saving 1
	June 12	Motor dinghy, gave help
	July 24	Motor boat DAWN MIST, in tow of fishing boat, escorted
	Aug 2	Man fallen from cliff, landed injured man, saving 1
	Aug 14	Yachts SAKURA and GAY PHILI, gave help
	Aug 14	Various yachts, landed 30
	Aug 20	Two dinghies, gave help. Escorted
	Aug 20	Y.C. rescue boat SULLY QUEEN, gave help. Escorted

	Oct 1	Sailing dinghy MAZIMA, gave help
1972	May 31	Bather, saved
	June 17	Two small boats, escorted
	June 25	Sailing dinghy LUCY LUCY, gave help
	June 29	Youths cut off by tide, saved 2
	Aug 7	Cabin cruiser APOLLO XV, escorted
	Aug 13	Cardigan Inshore Life-boat, saved boat
	Aug 20	Yacht, gave help. Persons stranded on rocks, saved 3
	Oct 22	Yacht HEPZIBHEL, saved 1
1973	June 20	Yacht RUM TUN, gave help
	Aug 8	Bathers, saved 4
	Aug 25	Persons cut off by tide, saved 3
	Sept 22	Motor yacht DOLPHIN, saved boat and 2
1974	June 21	Small boat, saved boat and 2
	July 14	Yacht CHRISTOPHER, saved yacht and 4
	July 29	Inflatable boat, saved 2.
	July 29	Motor fishing boat YNYS LOCHTYN, of Aberystwyth, saved 1
	July 30	Outboard dinghy, saved 1
	July 31	Yacht VIVA, gave help
1975	May 25	Persons stranded by tide, landed 16 (also 4 dogs)
	May 27	Persons stranded on cliff ledge, landed 5
	Jun.13	Speed-boat. saved boat

D-238

1976	Apr 22	Yacht, saved yacht and 1
	May 2	Motor boat, saved boat and 4
	May 16	Dinghy, saved dinghy and 2
	June 12	Speed-boat BOOMERANG, saved boat and 2
	June 13	Dinghy in tow, escorted vessels
	Aug 3	Missing person, landed 1
	Aug 19	Yacht MARCHOG, gave help
	Aug 19	Air-bed, saved 1
	Sept 9	Yacht UP SPIRITS, saved 2
	Sept 27	Sailing dinghy, gave help
1977	July 2	Speedboat, gave help
	Aug 3	Inflatable dinghy, saved dinghy and 2
	Aug 18	Saved a man from a cliff, 1
	Aug 26	Inflatable dinghy, saved dinghy and 1
1978	July 26	Three canoes, escorted
	Aug 16	Dinghy, saved dinghy and 3
	Aug 19	Sailing dinghy, saved dinghy and 1
	Aug 26	Fishing Boat WINNER, gave help
	Oct 31	Stood by for 2 stranded on cliffs
1979	Aug 17	Sailing dinghy, gave help
	Aug 29	Gave help for man over cliff
	Sept 16	Speed boat WIZARD, gave help
1980	June 15	Motor cruiser, saved cruiser & 2
	July 15	DUNBAR CASTLE 2 and DUNBAR CASTLE 3. Landed 28

	Aug 3	Skin diver, gave help
	Aug 10	Rubber dinghy, landed 2
	Aug 10	Speedboat in tow, escorted
	Aug 15	Sailing dinghy, gave help
	Aug 17	Rowing boat, saved boat and 2
	Sept 7	Powered boat, landed 6 and saved boat
	Oct 21	Speedboat, saved boat & 2
1981	July 1	Rowing boat Craft saved - nobody aboard
	Aug 10	Large open powered boat
	Aug 15	Person cut off by tide Persons landed
	Aug 24	Fishing vessel (small) ill crewman on vessel. Persons landed
1982	July 6	Small powered boat. Dead body, Body landed
	Aug 6	Sailing dinghy Capsize Craft saved - nobody aboard
1983	July 10	Sailing dinghy. Adverse conditions, others assisted
	July 10	Small powered boat with cabin. Machinery failure. Craft brought in
	July 20	Bather/swimmer. Person missing, gave help
	Aug 6	Inflatable dinghy. Vessel abandoned, derelict or adrift. Craft brought in
1984	May 10	Person cut off by tide In danger of being carried away by tide Gave help - not elsewhere specified
	July 12	Large powered boat with cabin. ill crewman. Persons landed
	Aug 19	Small open powered boat Adverse conditions Craft brought in - nobody aboard
	Aug 26	Sailboard. Adverse conditions Persons & craft saved
	Aug 28	Inflatable dinghy Adverse conditions Persons & craft saved 2
1985	May 25	Sailboard. Adverse conditions, others assisted

	Aug 27	Sailboard. Adverse conditions, person and craft saved
	Aug 27	Inflatable dinghy. Adverse conditions, 2 persons & craft saved
1986	Aug 1	Sailing dinghy capsize. Persons saved 4
	Sept 1	Sailboard. Adverse conditions. Persons & craft saved

D-339

1987	Aug 7	Sailing dinghy capsize. Persons & craft saved 1
	Aug 13	Rowing boat. Adverse conditions. Persons & craft saved 2
1988	June 28	Large powered boat. Machinery failure. Craft brought in - nobody aboard
	July 29	Small open powered boat. Fire. Persons saved 1
	Aug 11	Small powered boat, machinery failure. Persons & craft saved 4
	Aug 12	Inflatable dinghy. Adverse conditions. Persons & craft saved 1
	Aug 13	Sailboard. Adverse conditions. Persons & craft saved
	Aug 20	Sailboard. Adverse conditions. Persons & craft saved
	Aug 21	Sailboard. Adverse conditions. Persons & craft saved 2
	Sept 1	Small powered boat. Machinery failure. Persons & craft saved 3
1989	Mar 26	Small powered boat with cabin. Swamping. Persons saved 1
	Mar 30	Sailing dinghy. Adverse conditions. Persons & craft saved 1
	June 11	Sailing dinghy capsize .Persons & craft saved 1
	June 11	Inflatable dinghy capsize. Persons & craft saved 1
	Aug 16	Sailboard. Adverse conditions. Persons & craft saved 1
	Aug 19	Sailboard. Adverse conditions. Person & craft saved
	Sept 17	Sailboard. Adverse conditions. Persons & craft saved 1

1990	June 29	Person cut off by tide In danger of being carried away. 2 saved
	June 30	Sailboard. Adverse conditions. Persons & craft saved 1
	June 30	Sailing dinghy capsize. Persons & craft saved 1
	Aug 19	Fishing vessel. Machinery failure Person& craft saved 1
	Aug 20	Sailing dinghy Capsize Escorted a vessel 0
	Sept 16	Persons cut off by tide. In danger of being carried away. saved 2
1991	July 5	Sailing dinghy Adverse conditions Persons & craft saved 2
	July 18	Inflatable dinghy Leaks / Swamping Craft saved
1992	Apr18	Sailboard, Sail failure / dismasting. Persons & craft saved 1
	Aug 1	Sail multihull (no engine) Capsize Persons saved 1
	Aug 9	Persons cut off by tide In danger of being carried away. saved 2
	Aug10	Inflatable dinghy Adverse conditions False alarm
	Aug12	Sailboard Adverse conditions Persons & craft saved 1
	Aug12	Air bed / surfboard Adverse conditions Persons & saved 2
	Aug12	Air bed /surfboard Adverse conditions Persons & craft saved 2
1993	Aug 23	Sailing dinghy Capsize ˙persons landed
	Sept 25	Sail yacht (no engine) ill crewman on board. Persons landed
1994	June 1	Three persons cut off by tide. Gave help.
	June 2	Boy fallen from cliffs. Gave help.
	June 18	Rubber dinghy. One life and boat saved
	July 25	Sail board. One life and board saved
	Aug 19	Person fallen from cliffs. One life saved
		In addition, the lifeboat launched on a further 4 occasions
1995	May 1	Cabin cruiser BLACK PRINCE. 2 persons and craft brought in

D-476 Corydd

	May 7	Rubber dinghy LION HEART. Four persons and craft
	June 8	Rubber dinghy brought. Two persons landed. craft brought in
	June 22	Woman in sea. Gave help
	Aug 27	Dinghy. Two lives saved
		In addition, the lifeboat launched on a further 4 occasions
1996	Apr 17	Fishing vessel. Gave help
	June 12	Hang-glider. Gave help
	Aug 22	Catamaran.Two persons landed and craft saved
	Aug 26	Motor boat MAYBE. Six persons and craft brought in
	Oct 5	Sailing dinghy. Two persons landed and craft saved
		In addition, the lifeboat launched on a further 3 occasions
1997	Feb 6	Motor vehicle in sea. Stood by
	May 28	Man cut off by tide. One life saved
	May 28	Motor boat LADY ELEANOR. Escorted craft
	June 29	Two men stranded on cliffs. Two people brought in
	July 29	Two sailboards.Two people landed and two boards brought in
	Aug 6	Dinghy. Three lives saved
	Sept 5	Catamaran. Three lives and craft saved
	Oct 4	Sailing dinghy. Craft brought in.
		In addition, the lifeboat launched on a further 7 occasions
1998	June 14	Dinghy in tow of sailing club rescue craft. Escorted craft
	June 20	Sailing dinghy. Two people landed and craft brought in
	Aug 22	Two youths cut off by tide. Two lives saved
	Aug 30	Inflatable dinghy. Two people and craft brought in

		In addition, the lifeboat launched on a further 6 occasions
1999	May 22	Boy cut off by tide. One person brought in
	May 30	Jet ski. Escorted jet ski
	June 20	Motor boat. Three lives and craft saved
	July 27	Yacht. Six lives and craft saved
	Aug 9	Sailing dinghy. Two people landed and craft brought in
	Aug 14	Person injured. One person brought in
	Aug14	Sailing dinghy. Two people landed and craft brought in
	Aug 16	Person injured. Gave help
	Aug 17	Angling vessel DUNBAR CASTLE 3. 10 people, craft brought in
	Aug 24	Six people cut off by tide. Six people brought in
	Aug 27	Person injured. Gave help
		In addtion, the lifeboat launched on a further 2 occasions
2000	Feb 19	Two people cut off by the tide. Gave help
	Apr 28	Sheep. Gave help
	May 13	Nine stranded on rocks. Nine people brought in
	June 17	Sailing dinghy. One person and craft brought in
	July 22	Sailing dinghy. One person landed and craft brought in
	July 31	Sailing dinghy. Two people and craft brought in
	Aug 5	Inflatable dinghy. One person landed and craft brought in
		In addtion, the lifeboat launched on a further 6 occasions
2001	May 11	Two people stranded on rocks. Two people landed
	July 1	Two people stranded on rocks. Two people landed
	July 23	Fourteen people cut off by the tide. Fourteen lives saved
	July 30	Speedboat. Four lives and a dog saved
	Aug 5	Speedboat GWYLAN. Four people and craft brought in

	Aug 7	Sailing dinghy. Escorted craft
	Aug 7	Sailing dinghy. Two people and craft brought in
	Aug 19	Sailing dinghy. Two people landed and craft brought in
	Aug 31	Angler cut off by the tide. Stood by
	Sept 11	Speedboat BARBARA ANN. Two people and craft brought in
	Oct 21	Speedboat MOR FERLEN. Three people and craft brought in
		Additionally, the lifeboat launched on a further 5 occasions
2002	Mar 9	Two people cut off by the tide. Two people landed
	May 28	Person fallen on cliff path. One person landed
	June 1	Six people cut off by the tide. Six people landed
	July 11	People stranded on rocks. Two people landed
	Aug 1	People stranded on rocks. Three people landed
	Aug14	People cut off by the tide Two people landed
	Aug 29	Sailboard. One person landed and board brought in
		Additionally the lifeboat launched on a further 5 occasions
2003	Apr 17	People stranded on rocks. Two people landed
	Aug 5	People stranded. Gave help
	Aug 11	Kayaks. Two people and craft brought in
	Aug 29	People in the sea. Stood by
	Sept 1	Person in the sea. One life saved
		Additionally, the lifeboat launched on a further 3 occasions.
2004	Jan 25	Missing person. Landed a body

D-616 Amy Lea

	May 27	Powered boat SEA SPRAY. Four people and craft brought in
	June 2	Person cut off by tide at Gilfach Yr Halen. 1 person & dog landed
	July 10	Powered boat. Two people and craft brought in
	July 29	Injured person. Gave help - conveyed ambulance personnel. Stood by
	Aug 7	Catamaran. Gave help - righted catamaran
	Aug 13	Injured person. One person landed
	Aug 28	Injured person. One person brought in
		Additionally, the lifeboat launched on a further 4 occasions
2005	May 4	Swimmer in difficulties. One person landed
	June 12	Injured person. One person landed
	June 20	Fishing vessel dismasting. Person and craft brought in
	July 12	Small powered boat. Four people and craft brought in
	Aug 1	Person on cliffs cut off by tide. One person brought in
	Aug 14	Dinghy. Man overboard. One person landed
	Oct 4	Persons cut off by tide. 2 people brought in
		Additionally the lifeboat launched on a further 6 occasions
2006	Apr 14	Dog. One person and dog brought in
	May 28	People cut off by tide.Two people and two dogs brought in
	June 10	Inflatable dinghy. One person and craft brought in
	July 30	Sailing dinghy. Two people landed and craft brought in
	Aug 16	Sailing dinghy. Two people landed and craft brought in
	Aug 25	Kayaks. Two people and craft brought in
	Aug 25	Lifeguard on board. One person and craft brought in

	Oct 23	Dog. Landed a body
		Additionally, the lifeboat launched on a further 4 occasions
2007	Mar 2	Dogs at risk. Gave help
	Mar 21	Missing Person. Gave help
	Apr 25	Human body. Landed a body
	June 9	Powered boat MAD MAX. Four people and craft brought in
	June 29	Person in the sea. One life saved
	July 12	Gas bottle. Gave help
	Aug 21	Person in the sea. Gave help - transferred casualty to ALB
	Aug 22	Yacht ROCKABILLY. Three people and craft brought in
	Aug 26	Powered boat SEA WARRIOR. Gave help - took over tow
	Sept 3	Sailing dinghy. Two people and craft brought in
	Sept 24	Person in sea. Landed a body
	Dec 11	Dog. Stood by
		Additionally, the lifeboat launched on a further 6 occasions
2008	July 4	Yacht LAST LAUGH 2. Escorted craft
	July 12	Powered boat. Two people and craft brought in
	Aug 3	Canoe. Two people landed and craft brought in
	Aug 3	Powered boat WHISTLER. One person and craft brought in
	Oct 5	Fishing vessel BLUE PEARL. Gave help - freed propeller
	Oct 11	Human body. Landed a body
		Additionally, the lifeboat launched on a further 6 occasions
2009	Feb 11	Person on cliff. Gave help
	Apr 2	People cut off by tide. Five people brought in
	May 16	People in the sea. Gave help - transferred casualties to ALB
	June 28	Inflatable dinghy. Two people and craft brought in
	July 23	Fishing vessel CATHERINE ARDEN. Escorted craft

	July 28	Powered boat. Two people and craft brought in
	Aug 14	Injured child. One person landed
	Aug 14	People cut off by tide. Two people brought in
	Aug 18	Dog. Gave help - rescued dog
	Aug 28	Sailing dinghy. Five people landed and craf brought in
	Aug 30	Kayaks. 1 person landed and 3 people and kayaks brought in
	Sept 29	Catamaran WILD GOOSE 2. Gave help. Freed propeller
		Additionally, the lifeboat launched on a further 10 occasions
2010	Mar 26	Sailing dinghy. One person and craft brought in
	Apr 15	Flares. Gave help
	May 15	Dog. Gave help - rescued dog
	May 20	People cut off by tide. Two people brought in
	June 21	Person in the sea. One life saved
	July 23	Person cut off by tide. One person landed
	July 28	Yacht MAID MOIRA. Gave help - refloated casualty
	Sept 4	Powered boat. Stood by
	Sept 30	Person cut off by tide. One person and dog landed
	Oct 8	Catamaran OCEAN PROWLER. Gave help - secured casualty
	Oct 29	Tender. 2 people landed and craft brought in
		Additionally, the lifeboat launched on a further 4 occasions
2011	Jan 24	Fishing vessel GRATITUDE. Gave help, secured casualty
	Mar 26	People cut off by tide. 11 people landed
	Apr 15	People cut off by tide. 3 people brought in
	Apr 22	Powered boat ASOKE TANO. 7 people and craft brought in.
	June 2	People cut off by tide. 6 people landed
	June 14	Person at risk on cliff. One life saved
	June 14	Kayak. One life saved, one person landed and craft saved

	June 25	Sailing dinghy. 2 people and craft brought in
	July 28	Swimmers. Gave help
	Sept 26	Fishing vessel SANDERLING. 3 people and craft brought in
	Sept 27	Injured man at Ynys Lochtyn. Gave help, administered first aid
	Dec 21	Fishing vessel CATHERINE ARDEN. Gave help
		Additionally, the lifeboat launched on a further 11 occasions
2012	May 16	Person on rocks. 1 person landed
	May 25	Airbed/Dinghy. 2 people and craft brought in
	July 22	Person on rocks cut off by tide. 5 people landed
	July 22	Canoe/Kayak Gave help
	Aug 3	Powered boat. 2 people, 1 dog and craft brought in
	Aug 30	Person in water in danger of drowning. 1 life saved

D-754 Audrey LJ

	Sept 16	Powered boat SUMMER WINE. Assistance given
	Sept 22	Powered boat out of fuel. 3 people and craft brought in
	Dec 13	Fishing vessel PIONEER. Gave help
		Additionally, the lifeboat launched on a further 11 occasions
2013	Apr 3	Yacht with engine DAVICO. Gave help
	Apr 28	Yacht with engine GOLDEN CLOUD. 2 people & craft brought in
	May 4	Person on rocks. 2 people landed
	May 26	Person on rocks. 3 people landed
	June 5	Fishing vessel SANDERLING. Gave help
	June 24	Person on rocks cut off by tide. 4 people landed
	July 17	Fishing vessel DUNBAR CASTLE 2. Gave help, administered first aid

	July 22	Rowing boat. Escorted to safety
	July 27	Powered boat. Gave help, administered first aid
	July 31	Person on rocks. 1 person landed
	Aug 5	Powered boat. Gave help
	Aug 17	Sailing dinghy. Gave help
	Aug 17	Sailing dinghy. 2 people and craft brought in
	Aug 26	Canoe/Kayak. 1 person and craft brought in
	Sept 8	Person on rocks. 2 people landed
	Sept 8	Powered boat. 2 people and craft brought in
		Additionally, the lifeboat launched on a further 7 occasions
2014	Jan 3	Person on rocks. Gave help

Coxswains

1864 not recorded
1875 E.M.Davies
1880 Owen Evans
1905 David Davies
1918 Frederick Shaylor
1935 David Evans
1936 James Garfield Williams
1947 Arden Evans
1958 D. Rhosland Davies
1965 Winston Evans
1994 Daniel Potter

Mechanics

1947 Gwilym Davies
1965 Sydney Fowler
1975 Mervyn Thomas
2001 Richard Wood
2008 Ben Billingham